AUTONOMOUS TRANSFORMATION

AUTONOMOUS TRANSFORMATION

CREATING A MORE HUMAN FUTURE IN THE
ERA OF ARTIFICIAL INTELLIGENCE

Brian Evergreen

WILEY

For general information on our other products and services or for technical support, please contact our Customer Care Department within the United States at (800) 762-2974, outside the United States at (317) 572-3993 or fax (317) 572-4002.

Wiley also publishes its books in a variety of electronic formats. Some content that appears in print may not be available in electronic formats. For more information about Wiley products, visit our web site at www.wiley.com.

Library of Congress Cataloging-in-Publication Data is Available:

ISBN 9781119985297 (Cloth)
ISBN 9781119985310 (ePDF)
ISBN 9781119985303 (epub)

Cover Design: Wiley
Cover Image: © Dmitry Vinogradov/Shutterstock
Author photo: © Marissa Siebert

SKY10048967_061223

For Audrey—you are all the gardens I have ever gazed at, longing.
For Leo, my golden sun and the brightest morning.
For Aila, my moon and stars.

CONTENTS

Introduction: We Can Create a More Human Future

Since the invention of the Internet, technology has been one of, if not the most powerful change agent in existence. We have all borne witness to the changes, for better and for worse, that technology has had on society, our nations, our cities, the nature of work, and the human experience. In the era of artificial intelligence, together with its adjacent technologies, the rate of change is accelerating, and the impacts are yet to be determined.

This is a book for people who want to create a better future within this context of change. Some may have picked up this book hoping it will answer the question of why so few artificial intelligence initiatives succeed and provide a better way. Others may be interested in creating a better future for the front-line workers in their organization through the implementation of technology, empowering them with the latest tools and technologies, improving the experience of their work, and increasing job security and compensation. Others may be looking to lead a full-scale Autonomous Transformation across their organization to reimagine their organization's function in the broader market and communities they serve and are intrigued at the seemingly counterintuitive prospect of creating a more human future through the implementation of the latest technologies. Others may be starting their career or still trying to determine the right career trajectory, and hope this book can inform that process. Others might be reading this book to learn more about a loved one who works in technology or because they find technology interesting and want to hear about what shape the future might take.

If you are looking at this book for any of those reasons, you are in the right place. The principles, frameworks, and methods in these pages have been designed from experience across industries and geographies and at the highest levels of organizations, sharpened and given color through discussions and stories shared by leaders across the private and public sectors, academia, and research institutes as means of directing purposeful change in the face of technological upheavals in the context of systems that were built to be maintained—not changed (more on that later).

This journey began with a series of questions: Why do only 13% of data science initiatives make it into production?[1] Why do domain experts, technologists, and business leaders seem to be consistently embattled internally when they share common goals? Does that have anything to do with the social divides in society? If corporate leaders are greedy capitalists, why are so many trying to make the world a better place? And why are so many of those efforts and investments failing? Everyone keeps talking about machines taking jobs; is that happening? If so, where and how should we react as leaders and as a society? If not, why is it such a key theme discussed in our culture?

The answers to these questions led to more questions but also a thread of seemingly disconnected answers, which I pulled as hard as I could, like the thread of a sweater. This book is a collection of what I found in the unravelings, combined with my own experience leading and advising Digital Transformation initiatives for some of the world's most valuable companies and trying to solve systemic challenges together, using the best and latest technologies paired with immense resources. I have translated these findings into the principles, frameworks, and methods with which organizational leaders can create a more human future in this era of change.

What Is a More Human Future?

If this book succeeds in its aim of equipping you with the process by which you might influence or even create the future in the context of technological upheaval, there remains the question of what future you will create.

If your goal is similar to mine, in that you want to create a more human future and have a positive impact on humanity or even simply on the humans around you, it will be important to start with a shared understanding and definition of what a more human future could look like and what kind of future impacts would be positive for humankind so that you can communicate that goal effectively with others and measure your impacts against that goal.

This definition will inevitably vary across geographic and cultural backgrounds, but the following posits a starting point from which individuals or organizational leaders can build a vision for their definition of a more human future:

For me, a more human future is one in which future generations have the capability to be safe and healthy, to have access to rich educational experiences, to connect meaningfully with other people from all over the world, to make and purchase ethically sourced goods, to have dignity through both the access and the ability to create value in the world and be compensated fairly, to look forward to the future with hope, to feel empowered to create a better future for their future generations, to delight in the vastness of the human experience across cultures and history, to deeply understand and feel empowered to make ethical choices without the presence of bias, implicit or otherwise, and to harness their uniquely human potential to do or be or create something that is meaningful to them.

How Do We Create This More Human Future?

In the absence of a design and purposeful direction to create a better, more human future by leaders (like you), technological change will follow the path of the existing systems and processes in the world. The relationship between humans and machines, strained as it is, will become more strained. Work that has been dehumanized will become less human or be replaced entirely by mechanized systems. The most advanced technologies, capable of immense positive impact on the world, will continue to be nearly impossible to implement, and therefore only be available to those who have a significant amount of capital, and then only because its use has been justified as a means of generating more profit. This is not a disparagement of the people who lead the organizations that shape our world and our day-to-day experience; rather, it is pointing at train tracks and suggesting that, without a significant degree of effect and redesign of those tracks, the inbound train will follow the same trajectory, regardless of who is at the helm.

These challenges can be daunting. If any of them were simple to fix, they would already have been resolved. The investments in executives and their teams discussing partnership, brainstorming, and developing charters and proposing initiatives to resolve these challenges that have subsequently not moved forward, paired with the low rate of success for technological initiatives leveraging artificial intelligence and its adjacent emerging technologies, paints a bleak picture.

Fortunately, these challenges can be addressed, with positive impacts to our organizations, the people working within them, the communities they serve and in which they operate, and to society. How? By replacing the way that we approach solving problems.

This is one of the surprising findings that has led to writing this book. Eighty-seven percent of organizational leaders who have applied the best processes (or approaches to solving problems) available to them to implement machine learning, a subdiscipline of artificial intelligence, have been unsuccessful. *The best processes available to them.* We have inherited and optimized processes and systems designed in the Industrial Revolution that have been instrumental in architecting and solving twentieth-century challenges. Unfortunately, however, with the dramatic increase of complexity in the twenty-first century, these processes are no longer effective at leveraging the newest technologies.

These challenges with how we approach technology and the issues we face as a society are more intertwined than would appear at the surface, which will be demonstrated throughout this book. For now, I will share the blueprint this book will endeavor to provide leaders with to create a more human future through the successful implementation of artificial intelligence and the other technologies (Internet of Things, digital twins/simulations, robotics, and mixed reality) that comprise Autonomous Transformation.

The process of Autonomous Transformation to create a more human future is shown in Figure I.1.

Creating a more human future is not a proposed end product or byproduct of this process, nor is it a lofty aspiration. Rather, it is a practical element applied in each step of the above process, as will be examined in each section of the book.

In other words, if you have picked up this book in hopes of finding practical insights about applying artificial intelligence and its connected technologies and think the idea of creating a more human future sounds like, for lack of a better word, "fluff," this is still the book for you, and the important point I want to share with you is that creating a more human future is a practical component of *how* we implement artificial intelligence and its connected technologies—it is not an outcome at the end of the process, but integral to every step, as I will demonstrate throughout the book.

The first component of this is Profitable Good.

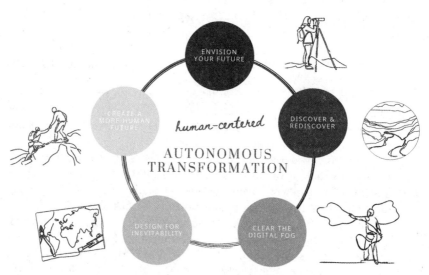

Figure I.1   The Autonomous Transformation Process

What Is Profitable Good?

Profitable Good is an equation: ***Profit + [positive human impact]***.

In this equation, profit retains its standard definition, the net difference between the cost of goods and the price at which goods are sold, and is combined with an outcome that positively impacts the human experience. The following three market signals demonstrate the strategic need for Profitable Good.

1. Talent Preferences

An organization's alignment or misalignment with people's values is affecting not only where they are willing to spend their money, but where they are willing to work. Numerous reports have demonstrated that Generation Z employees will leave an organization when its actions do not align with their values.[2]

In the twenty-first-century talent market, where the Internet has extended both awareness and access of the proliferation of available jobs, required skills, and even the ability to directly connect with people working at those companies, the ability to be more effective in hiring and retaining competitive talent is essential, and among the most effective strategies for accomplishing this is creating a dynamic where the fundamental accrual of employees' work aligns with their values.

2. Market Preference (e.g., doing good has become an economic force)

According to a recent Ernst & Young survey, 90% of global institutional investors revise investments if companies do not at least consider environmental or social responsibility within their business model.[3]

Many individuals use their spending power as a means of holding companies accountable for poor corporate practices related to these causes, while nearly half of all consumers in the United States have boycotted a company whose actions they deemed detrimental to society. Conversely, buyers also choose to reward businesses they believe are doing social or environmental good, as evidenced by a recent finding that revenue from sustainable products is growing at six times the rate of other products.[4,5]

3. Strategic Partner Preference

More and more, organizations are seeing the benefit of developing an ecosystem of strong partners, honing their core competencies, and aligning with organizations that share the same goals. Partnerships can be formed on the basis of shared goals that are merely fiscal or focused on market–product fit, but the longevity and depth of partnerships based on goals aligned to the values of leaders and of the organizational cultures that attracted talent to those organizations in the first place are much more likely to last and to thrive.

Profitable Good is more difficult to achieve than profit alone, but will be an important differentiator for organizations in the era of Autonomous Transformation, as 87% of customers would switch from a less socially responsible brand to a more socially responsible competitor. This is evident in the success of The Honest Company, an entrant into a crowded bath, beauty, and home goods market that prices goods at a premium over competitors in exchange for socially responsible sourcing, creation, and sales of their goods. The Honest Company went public in 2021, valued at $1.4 billion.[6]

Practically, if an organization started a new initiative today to use artificial intelligence to reduce cost on the production of a product that is not good for the environment, it would face challenges related to all three of these categories: for example, data scientists (*talent*), who have a broad range of career options due to the imbalance of data scientists to organizations that wish to implement artificial intelligence, are statistically less likely to join or stay with the organization to fulfill the goal of that initiative. Even if that challenge were overcome and the initiative led to implementation and a successful reduction of cost, the outlook of return on investment is low, as increasing market awareness of how products are impacting the environment leads to boycotting products and companies, which could very likely impact this organization and product. Lastly, partnerships from technology companies and consulting firms are actively reviewed through the lens of societal good, from a perspective of both purpose as well as the return on investment, as helping a customer or client reduce cost on a product that is not good for the environment is not something that could be leveraged by the technology or consulting firm's marketing departments to demonstrate the quality of their technology or services and also poses the risk of negative press.

Greed, Profit, and Altruism

The naming convention of Profitable Good raises questions regarding the merit of profit, particularly in the current environment, in which *profit* is used interchangeably, or at least in the same breath, as *greed*.

Profit is not the same thing as altruism, and it is also not the same as greed.

Political economists have been working for years to reimagine our economic systems, but as it stands, the organizations that wield the greatest potential to create a better, more human future are reliant on profit.

This includes not only the obvious, such as for-profit organizations, but also nonprofit organizations, governments, academic institutions, and research institutions—every organization is reliant on profit.

This is admittedly a polarizing statement. In the contemporary global discourse, profit has become synonymous with greed, but incorrectly so. Profit and greed can and do coexist, but they are not the same.

For those who require evidence to support the claim that every organization is reliant on profit: nonprofit organizations are funded, through donations, by for-profit organizations, the people who work for them, and government grants. Governments are funded primarily by taxes and tariffs (e.g., 97% of the United States' federal revenue in 2022),[7] paid by for-profit organizations and people who work for them. Academic institutions are funded largely by governments and by tuition paid for by families who work for for-profit organizations or by nonprofit organizations, which are funded by for-profit organizations, by governmental agencies, which are funded by for-profit organizations and the people who work for them, and so on.

Ergo, if all for-profit organizations and the people who worked for them left the United States overnight, the nation would have a fixed date by which no new initiatives could be funded—no streets would be repaired, no students would be able to attend college, and no new funding would flow into nonprofits or research institutes—not to mention the inevitable shortage of food and goods.

This is a symbiotic interdependency, as without governments, academic institutions, research institutions, or nonprofit organizations, for-profit organizations would not be able to exist or thrive, as they would lack the necessary infrastructure, protection, talent, and underlying technological and scientific breakthroughs, to name a few. This is made evident by an examination of the concentration of successful startups in technology around the world, in which there is a correlation found between the number of successful startups and the governmental and education context in which they are founded.

The technical definition of profit is the net difference between the cost of goods and the price at which goods are sold.

Taxes are included in the cost of goods, so when examining profit through the lens of the function it serves in the broader system, it is the post-tax incentive for creating something deemed valuable enough by someone else that they chose to purchase it at that price.

At the individual level, that incentive can outweigh the risk of starting something new, and is a key driving element for innovation and gainful employment.

At the manager or director level, the ability to contribute more value to the organization than the cost of the team and its spend in a given year can determine whether a team grows or is subject to restructuring or layoffs.

At the organizational level, organizations are like ecosystems, and profit is the water that nourishes the organization. If you remove water from an ecosystem, it will no longer be able to sustain life. Likewise, if an organization is no longer profitable, it will need to either be funded by other organizations that have remained profitable, funded by government bailouts, or it will need to close its doors, eliminating jobs as well as its ability to create value.

Profitable Good, in the context of greed, profit, and altruism, can be examined in Figure I.2. This visualization illustrates the neutrality of profit, which is inherently neither greedy nor altruistic. There are organizations in which money is pursued at any cost, the cost of which is usually humanity, that fall on the greed end of the scale. Likewise, there are organizations in which good is pursued at any cost, the cost of which is money, and therefore are reliant on charitable donations from for-profit organizations and from individuals who have a surplus of funds they or their predecessors have accumulated through profit.

Examination of this scale begs two questions: Should all organizations be designed for altruism? And if not, why not design all organizations for profitable good?

The answer lay in the function the organization serves in the market and society, and the two simplest determining factors are whether the need is ongoing, and whether there is a natural path to generating a profit. If the need is short-term, such as a natural disaster, there is not a logical path to creating profit that also serves the mission of aiding in disaster relief. In the case of starting a company that creates compostable packaging that could be sold to consumer packaged goods companies, however, the need is ongoing, and there is a natural space in which to generate a profit.

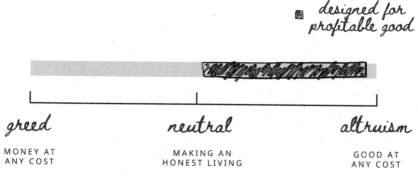

Figure I.2   Measuring Profitable Good

What About Social Purpose Corporations?

There are many different routes a corporation could take in terms of its legal structure to indicate its intention to make the world a better place. Autonomous Transformation is a vehicle for achieving those goals. For any kind of organization, Autonomous Transformation is an opportunity to create a more human future regardless of its legal status.

Profitable Good in the Real World

If a researcher at a technology company developed a method that could significantly reduce the carbon emissions of a building, that company would be incented by both profit and the prospect of doing good to invest in incubating, testing, and productizing that development. Furthermore, mutually beneficial partnerships could be formed with that organization's entire external ecosystem within that domain, such as building management system companies, systems integrators, and facilities management organizations. Every organization involved is incented to sell this solution to customers, who are incented to buy it and therefore reduce cost and emissions, and carbon emissions around the world are reduced.

A second example of Profitable Good is taking place in the United States, where research is being funded by the Advanced Robotics for Manufacturing Institute and the National Science Foundation to address technology and workforce gaps in the U.S. fishing industry. Currently, fish caught off the East Coast of the United States are shipped abroad to be thawed, processed, and chemically treated before being returned for distribution. This process is costly, time-consuming, and leads to a higher risk of contamination.

By developing a robotic system that can reliably handle seafood while working collaboratively with human workers, the profit/labor cost equation can be balanced, and these fish can be processed domestically, which is better for consumers and creates jobs back in the United States, not only for the human workers in the factories, but also for mechanical engineers and plant leadership.[8]

As a society, we are not going to stumble into a more human future, especially as we navigate technological upheaval. The prospect of the value of applying artificial intelligence and its adjacent technologies combined with the impossibility of their application without reevaluating and redesigning our organizations creates an opportunity to anchor on Profitable Good and design a more human future. This book aspires to give you all that you need to get started.

Notes

1. VB Staff, "Why Do 87% of Data Science Projects Never Make It into Production?," *Venture-Beat*, July 19, 2019, https://venturebeat.com/ai/why-do-87-of-data-science-projects-never-make-it-into-production (accessed January 15, 2023).
2. J. Wingard, "'The Great Resignation': Why Gen Z Is Leaving the Workforce in Droves . . . and What to Do About It," *Forbes*, September 2, 2021, https://www.forbes.com/sites/jasonwingard/2021/09/02/the-great-resignation-why-gen-z-is-leaving-the-workforce-in-drovesand-what-to-do-about-it/?sh=df7257e5f870 (accessed March 12, 2023).
3. Ernst & Young Global Limited, Global Institutional Investor Survey 2018.
4. William H. Clark, Jr. and Elizabeth K. Babson, "How Benefit Corporations Are Redefining the Purpose of Business Corporations," *William Mitchell Law Review* 38, no. 2, article 8 (2012), http://open.mitchellhamline.edu/wmlr/vol38/iss2/8 (accessed March 12, 2023).
5. M. Tonello, T. Singer, and C. Mitchell, "The Business Case for Corporate Investment in Sustainable Practices," ICCR Institute, 2015.
6. E. Wang, "Jessica Alba-Backed Honest Company IPO Raises $412.8 mln," *Reuters*, May 4, 2021, https://www.reuters.com/business/retail-consumer/jessica-alba-backed-honest-company-ipo-raises-4128-million-2021-05-04 (accessed March 12, 2023).
7. Fiscal Data, "How Much Revenue Has the U.S. Government Collected This Year?," U.S. Treasury, 2023, https://fiscaldata.treasury.gov/americas-finance-guide/government-revenue/ (accessed March 24, 2023).
8. Advanced Robotics for Manufacturing, "ARM FISH Project Receives Additional NSF Funding," press release, October 3, 2019.

PART ONE
The Fundamentals

I believe that there is one story in the world, and only one. . . .
Humans are caught—in their lives, in their thoughts, in their hungers
and ambitions, in their avarice and cruelty, and in their kindness and
generosity too—in a net of good and evil. . . . There is no other story.
A [person], after [brushing] off the dust and chips of [. . .] life, will
have left only the hard, clean questions: Was it good or was it evil?
Have I done well—or ill?

—JOHN STEINBECK, *EAST OF EDEN*

CHAPTER 1

Reformation, Transformation, and Creation: Defining Autonomous Transformation

au·ton·o·mous \ ȯ-ˈtä-n·mous \ *adjective*
1: having the right or power of self-government
2: existing or capable of existing independently[1]

trans·for·ma·tion \ ˌtran(t)s-fər-ˈmā-shən \ *noun*
1: an act, process, or instance of transforming or being transformed
(*verb*): to change in composition or structure[2]

Autonomous Transformation, on the surface, could sound to many like the final process by which all work will be automated.

Although it does involve systems that can operate autonomously, which for many invokes concern about the elimination of jobs, Autonomous Transformation is instead the transformation of jobs across all verticals and levels, increasing the autonomy of human workers—that is to say, the right or power of self-government, existing or capable of existing independently.

Human autonomy and machine autonomy are two halves of the same coin, incapable of existing without one another in the context of the twenty-first century. The process of breaking tasks down into individual work elements that can be either automated or assigned to humans was, conceivably, the only path to meeting the demand for production placed on systems and organizations in the late nineteenth century and throughout the twentieth century. And as long as there are repetitive tasks that cannot be learned by or taught to machines, humans will need to operate those tasks.

With autonomous technologies, this is no longer the case. Networks of repetitive tasks previously too complex to be automated can now be learned by and taught to machines. This has the potential to transform the labor market and can be imagined as a new entrant to the pyramidal hierarchy of work, pushing humans upward from repetitive toward creative work—from operations toward stewardship.

This is a timely opportunity in the current macroeconomic climate because as organizations face recession, the desire to consider reshoring operations to harden supply chains against the risk of geopolitical and/or logistical challenges, and the loss of expertise as experts quit or retire, organizations need to do more with less, and Autonomous Transformation presents a time-sensitive opportunity to capture and extend human expertise to empower organizations to create more value with the same number of resources, ensuring business continuity and job stability.

Autonomous Transformation is the process of transforming an organization's products, services, processes, and structures through the reimagining and converting of analog and digital processes and assets to autonomous processes and assets.

A *human-centered* Autonomous Transformation carries the thread of the human experience of working within the organization together with the impact to the communities served by the organization through the process of transformation as a means of achieving Profitable Good as well as increasing the likelihood of successfully achieving and sustaining value creation through Autonomous Transformation.

As depicted in Figure 1.1, Digital Transformation is the process of transforming an organization's products, services, processes, and structures through the reimagining and converting of analog processes and assets to digital processes and assets.

This is not to be confused with Digital Reformation, which has been a prevalent market force under the guise of Digital Transformation since the coining of the term *Digital Transformation* in 2011.

> **ref·or·ma·tion** \ re-fər-ˈmā-shən \ *noun*
> **1: a:** to put or change into an improved form or condition
>   **b:** to amend or improve by change of form or removal of faults or abuses[3]

Digital Reformation is the process of reforming, or improving the performance of, an organization's products, services, processes, or structures through the conversion of analog processes and assets to digital processes and assets without changing the nature of those products, services, processes, or structures.

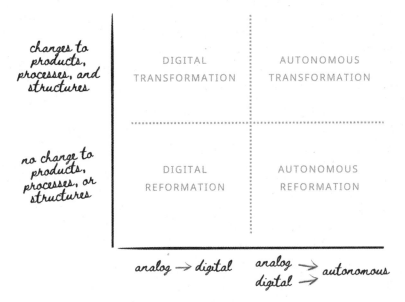

changes to products, processes, and structures

DIGITAL TRANSFORMATION

AUTONOMOUS TRANSFORMATION

no change to products, processes, or structures

DIGITAL REFORMATION

AUTONOMOUS REFORMATION

analog → digital   *analog → digital → autonomous*

Figure 1.1   Transformation and Reformation Matrix

Likewise, Autonomous Reformation is the process of reforming, or improving the performance of, an organization's products, services, processes, or structures through the converting of analog and digital processes and assets to autonomous processes and assets without changing the nature of those products, services, processes, or structures.

An example of Digital Transformation is Netflix's transition from solely sending DVDs in the mail to the invention of streaming. The core product and the processes and structures by which they delivered value to their customer base were reimagined and transformed within the digital paradigm, resulting in a ripple effect that is continuing to shape the trajectory of entertainment.

There are more examples of Digital Reformation than of Digital Transformation, such as within the airline industry. Booking with a travel agent has been largely replaced by booking with airlines or travel websites directly, which has significantly improved the customer experience, but the product, the process by which tickets are booked, and the structure of the airline are fundamentally the same. Checking into a flight has been significantly improved, or reformed, through the ability to check in online, but although the process of checking in has been improved through the converting of analog to digital, it has not been reimagined. Inside the airplane, paying with a credit card to make a phone call from one's seat has been reformed to paying with a credit card for Internet on one's device; the function and structure are the same, but the customer experience has been significantly improved.

An example of Autonomous Reformation is taking place at Bell Flight, where engineers have trained autonomous artificial intelligence agents to land drones based on a curriculum defined by pilots. In order to learn how to land autonomously, the artificial intelligence agent practiced landing in thousands of simulated scenarios every few minutes, thereby learning through experience plus expertise the same way a person learns. This is an important breakthrough, as drones with this capability can land without GPS or any type of radio or Internet signal, which means they can deliver vital medicine and other goods to communities in disaster scenarios, even if towers, roads, and pharmacies have been destroyed. This example is reformational and not transformational because the structure and process of the system itself have not been changed—they have been improved. This example does take a step in the direction of Autonomous Transformation, however, as drones that can land autonomously, together with the ability to take off, fly, recharge, change course, and so on could be leveraged to create transformational new products and services.[4]

There is not yet an example of a market-altering Autonomous Transformation, but there are several ventures in the direction of Autonomous Transformation, such as Amazon Go, a retail store without a checkout process because it recognizes its shoppers, personalizes their experiences, and uses their saved payment methods when they walk out of the store.

One could imagine this paradigm being applied to the airline industry, and the ability to walk in and set luggage directly onto a conveyor belt without needing to show identification or wait in line.

Another example in the direction of Autonomous Transformation is in the idea of the Internet of Things sensing when a consumer is low on a given product and making a purchase based on price-to-value and logistics. This has the capability to alter the advertising business, as machines are neither designed, nor have the capacity, to emotionally connect with advertisements, and would instead prioritize the best value in the required timing.

The example of Amazon Go illustrates autonomous technologies being leveraged to replace a current job category, whereas the example of the Internet of Things demonstrates the use of autonomous technologies to perform a new function that reduces the overall load on a human (in this case, the resident of the home). The third application of autonomous technologies is extending human capabilities, which can be described in the context of health care.

Health care is one of the most manual industries. Oversimplified, the process is to go speak with and show your symptoms to another person, who then performs a procedure, schedules tests, schedules procedures, prescribes treatment, and/or schedules a follow-up visit. The efficacy of the visit is reliant on the patient's ability to accurately convey their symptoms and family and personal medical history in a short time frame, sometimes as little as a 15-minute window, after waiting weeks or months. The demand for the human expertise of doctors dramatically outweighs the supply, resulting in disparity of access to health care and negatively impacting the performance of the health care system as a whole.

In the autonomous paradigm, this highly manual equation could be reimagined to extend the ability of medical practitioners to assist more people, with the potential to lower costs and create more access. An example of this would be the development of a digital twin of every patient that could be sharpened over time with every test, diagnosis, health event, procedure, and hospitalization. This would lay the foundation for faster diagnoses and triaging before a patient ever arrived at a hospital or clinic. In a visit, medical professionals could test treatment scenarios against the digital twin of the patient to verify the best treatment path, and augment their expertise by validating their proposed diagnoses and treatment with a system that had been trained with the expertise of hundreds, if not thousands, of medical experts and research papers, to recommend any other possible diagnoses and recommend tests or treatment plans, with analysis of the implications if they were wrong.

A fundamental capability this addresses that is not possible in today's paradigm is the systemic view of a patient, as even the most well-meaning practitioners often do not have time to stop and consider every test that could be taken or every subfield of medicine that could be examined to get to the root of a patient issue. A capability like this could leverage expertise across disciplines to recommend tests and treatment that could then be validated by a medical professional before being put into practice. This would benefit patients because they could have more frequent and holistic access to medical expertise, and it would benefit medical professionals because they could support more patients with the same or fewer resources, and their visits would be more targeted and informed with patient background and information.

Both reformation and transformation begin with something that exists, which is an inherent limitation when the system needs something that does not exist, such as in the health care example. These instances, which occur more often than is recognized, require acts of creation.

cre·a·tion \ krē-'ā-shən \ *noun*
1: the act of creating
   especially : the act of bringing the world into ordered existence
2: the act of making, inventing, or producing
3: something that is created[5]

Since its creation in 1861, the telephone has continuously been reformed and transformed. Multiplexing, which allowed several calls through the same telephone wire at the same time, is an example of reformation, and it introduced many times the efficiency. The touch-tone phone is an example of transformation, the cellular phone another transformation, and the smartphone yet another transformation—and since the invention and release of the smartphone, it has undergone a series of reformations.

But the smartphone would not have been possible if it were not for multiplexing, which laid the groundwork (pun intended) for cellular phones, together with a combination of creations, reformations, and transformations across many industry verticals, such as graphical computing, manufacturing capabilities, and scientific creations in batteries, chips, and scratch-resistant glass (to name a few), and compressed video and audio file formats.

In other words, a desired future outcome, such as a product release like the iPhone in 2007, is not the outcome of reformation, creation, or transformation taken individually. They are each processes, or means, with which to produce an outcome, and the leaders who harness the full potential of the technological and social systems of the twenty-first century will weave the three processes together, specific to their organization, market, and regulatory context, to arrive at a future point they have envisioned for their organization and/or for society.

Weaving Our Way to the Moon

The Jacquard loom, patented in 1804 by Jacques Marie Jacquard, was an invention that combined several preexisting inventions into a machine that made it possible for unskilled workers to weave fabrics with complex and detailed patterns in a fraction of the time it took a master weaver and an assistant working manually.

This development had important social and technological impacts. Before this invention, fashionable cloth was only accessible to the wealthiest in society. Now, such cloth adorned with intricate patterns could be mass-produced.

From a technological standpoint, the Jacquard loom laid the foundation on which computing and computer programming were developed. When Charles Babbage invented the first digital computer, the Analytical Engine, he used Jacquard's punch card concept. The punch card method developed by Jacquard persisted until the mid-1980s, and was used in the Apollo missions, as well as mainframe machines created by IBM. Ada Lovelace, the first computer programmer, became the world's only expert on the process of sequencing instructions on the punch cards that Babbage's Analytical Engine used, and famously said "The Analytical Engine weaves algebraic patterns, just as the Jacquard loom weaves flowers and leaves."[6]

Standing in front of one of the last working Jacquard looms, in the Henry Ford Museum of American Innovation, is a powerful experience, and the two-story machine is a looming physical representation of a creation that transformed a commodities market and, in doing so, laid the foundation for several steps of world-changing creation, reformation, and transformation.

History is filled with examples of the cycle of creation, reformation, and transformation, and the world needs creators, reformers, and transformers. Creators build new capability, whether it is a scientific breakthrough, a business model, a technology, a method, or a system. When that creation is introduced into the market, without a reformer to iterate on and improve the system, the value of the creation will be short-lived. Without transformers to reimagine the application of that creation across sectors or in combination with other creations, the creation will never drive systemic or worldwide value and society will not realize the full benefit or potential. Conversely, transformers need a steady supply of creations, stabilized through the process of reformation, as change agents with which to drive organizational and market transformation.

It should be noted that there is not and should be no value judgment inherent in these definitions and examples. For some organizations, reformational programs may be more attractive and a better fit for their risk tolerance or market position than for others. Individuals may find themselves attracted to and specializing in creation, reformation, or transformation, and leading organizations will need each of these functions and leaders who can facilitate and orchestrate the expertise and vision of these functions to achieve cross-organizational objectives.

Job Protectionism, Job Fatalism, and Job Pragmatism

The story of the Jacquard loom, viewed through the lens of the development of the computer, is innocuous and fascinating. Through the lens of the work landscape at the time, riots broke out in Lyon, France, attempts were made on Jacquard's life, and there were concerted efforts to destroy any Jacquard looms within the city limits.[7]

This is a historic example of a paradigm that these technologies and the title of this book are likely to first bring to mind, in which machines take over work that currently creates human jobs. Autonomous Transformation can and will be used to replace current human jobs, the same way that whalers lost jobs when oil lamps were invented and horse carriage drivers lost jobs when the automobile was invented, but forward-thinking leaders within those organizations and industries can plan ahead to ensure that those impacted by those changes are able to transition to other jobs within the organization and maintain steady employment.

In other words, within the amount of time and investment it takes to get a technology or group of technologies developed and integrated to the degree that they could reasonably handle all of the tasks currently handled by a human, there is ample time for the humans occupying those jobs to be informed of the coming changes, offered opportunities to train for other positions, and plan for a smooth transition to the next position within the organization.

This means that a sudden reduction of jobs due to automation or machine autonomy is the result of either a failure to plan, a failure to communicate, or an intentional choice to withhold information regarding a coming change.

In the wake of the Industrial Revolution, jobs have become equated with people, and it has become a value and symbol of integrity to be a proponent and/or agent of "job protectionism," or the belief that certain jobs or industries should be shielded from competition or other factors that may threaten their existence, even if this means sacrificing other economic or social goals.

Another philosophical lens through which the technology-fueled evolution of work and society is examined is "job fatalism," the belief that there is little or nothing that can be done to protect jobs or industries in the face of economic changes or competition. This view holds that the forces of globalization, technological advancement, or other factors are so powerful that they will inevitably lead to the loss of certain types of jobs or industries, regardless of any efforts to protect them.

Both of these beliefs are short-sighted and ill-suited for the era of artificial intelligence.

Job protectionism reduces competitiveness, as shielding jobs or industries from competition protects them in the short run but makes them less competitive in the long run, ultimately resulting in broader-sweeping job loss and harming economic growth.

Job fatalism can lead to a sense of resignation or hopelessness among leaders, workers, or policymakers, who may feel that there are no viable solutions to the challenges facing their communities or industries.

An alternative approach, "job pragmatism," examines the job market together with a belief that emphasizes practicality and effectiveness, rather than a dogmatic adherence to a particular ideology or principle. In the context of the future of the job market, a pragmatic approach would involve balancing the need to support existing jobs with the need to promote innovation, growth, and efficiency in the economy as a whole. This might involve measures such as targeted training and education programs, incentives for businesses to invest in new technologies and processes, and social safety nets to support workers during periods of transition or displacement.

It is the responsibility of organizational leaders to design workforce transformational strategies as an integral part of broader reformational and transformational strategies, and beginning with this consideration yields Profitable Good, preserving organizational legacy knowledge and expertise, engendering loyalty, and contributing to a healthy organizational culture.

Preservation of Human Work for Human Experiences

A world transformed and shaped by autonomy at all costs is a world devoid of basic human experiences that are inextricably tied to the nature of a product or service. Imagine a mall in which the only humans were the shoppers, or restaurants where only the diners were human. It would be dystopian.

Not all manual or transactional work is created equal. We are wired for human connection and although full autonomy could appear profitable in the short term, organizations that explore this will find that the market will rebound quickly in favor of organizations that retain human connection where it matters most. This has been demonstrated rigorously in the field of customer service.

In examining the potential of autonomous applications within an enterprise, organizations need to consider the customer and employee journey and expectations of their brand and their industry, both the minimum expectations to retain customers and employees, as well as opportunities to layer in human experiences to delight customers and increase customer and employee loyalty.

A customer may not leave a brand over having to wait in a virtual queue or not having a localized or personalized experience in the context of a support call, but they may be delighted by being greeted in their native language by a human customer service agent. Although this is not the core value proposition of the organization, the likelihood for consumers to stay or leave based on their emotional connection with a brand, driven by their access to and experiences with the humans who represent that brand, remains a critical input into the decision criteria and approach to autonomy. In the case where human connection is important, autonomous technologies can amplify the abilities of the human workers fulfilling those connection points with customers and employees.

Creating a More Human Future Through Creation, Reformation, and Transformation

If an organization is awarded the distinction of becoming the most digitally transformed organization in the world, but no one is buying their products and they cannot retain talent, Digital Transformation will have been a means to the wrong end.

Digitally transforming is only valuable if it is helping an organization achieve a specific goal it could not have achieved in the analog paradigm. Likewise with Autonomous Transformation and with acts of creation.

There are some organizations that would and will benefit from peeling back efforts to digitally transform where they see that customers preferred the analog experience, especially where it involved human connection. Here we will observe a form of "Analog Transformation."

If creation, reformation, and transformation are not goals, but processes by which to achieve outcomes, how do we define the right outcomes?

The first step is to determine a future point the organization would like to reach. This could be as simple as an improvement of profitability on a given product (which may only require the process of reformation), or as complex as creating a new market category.

Once the future point has been determined, as demonstrated in Figure 1.2, the organization can determine what would need to be true in order for the organization to reach that future point (more on this in Chapters 6 and 15), then determine which processes will be required to achieve these sets of objectives.

If the future point is determined to be a future in which no workers are harmed on the job in the context of a company that builds skyscrapers, what might have to be true could include analog outcomes, such as education of and adherence to a rigorous set of guidelines and processes by a workforce that involves a high degree of contractors and with varying first languages. Perhaps those educational resources have already been created but are not easy to access, so a digital reformation process is required along with providing tablets at job sites with many languages, with tracking mechanisms to ensure compliance. In parallel, depending on the largest contributors to workplace injuries, a combination of Digital Transformation, Autonomous Transformation, Autonomous Reformation, and creation initiatives could stitch together incremental decreases in workplace risk until the organization is able to reach its ultimate objective.

The steps of this process are represented in Figure 1.2, demonstrating how organizations that pivot from focusing solely on the process of transformation to the outcomes or the future they wish to manifest will significantly increase the likelihood of successful implementations and eliminating pilot purgatory. Furthermore, suborganizations, partnering together to achieve a mutual outcome, may undergo different processes in parallel. One department may undergo a Digital Reformation process to improve the quality of their data while another undergoes Autonomous Reformation to create digital twins of machinery—the two of which in combination create the foundation of a cross-organizational Autonomous Transformation initiative that represents the final phase of a strategy to reach a desired future state.

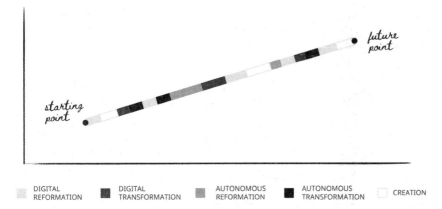

Figure 1.2   Reformation, Transformation, and Creation: The Path to the Future

Survivalism and Digital Darwinism

In the 25-year period from 1997 to 2022, 59% of Fortune 500 companies that were on the list fell off or went defunct. With this degree of sweeping impact on industries, many have, understandably, framed the need for Digital Transformation within the context of organizational existentialism and the need to survive the waves of change impacting the market.

This is absolutely true, but it is both dangerous and ultimately ineffective when it becomes the sole focus of an organization or its leaders.

The survival paradigm invokes fight, flight, or freeze, and can lead to short-term thinking and rash decisions. At its best, it is a well-intended means of making the case for change; at its worst, it is a sales tactic.

Regardless of the intention, a focus on survival is inherently self-interested. Organizations do not exist solely to benefit themselves, and they do not flourish when they are focused inward. Organizations thrive when they focus on creating customer value and treating their employees and customers well. If the leadership of an organization is solely asking the question of how to survive, how to beat the competition, or how to cut costs, it can be easy to lose sight of why the organization got into the business in the first place.

In the face of the era of artificial intelligence, there is an opportunity to pivot from organizational survival to the betterment of the human experience, both internal and external to the organization.

From a systems perspective, the organization is a part of a broader system and has an impact on the human experience. A reexamination of the organization's role within that broader system can illuminate how digital and autonomous capabilities can improve the organization's ability to deliver on its core value proposition to the betterment of society, which will ultimately enable the organization to thrive.

Notes

1. "Autonomous," Merriam-Webster Dictionary, https://www.merriam-webster.com/dictionary/autonomous.
2. "Transformed," Merriam-Webster Dictionary, https://www.merriam-webster.com/dictionary/transformed.
3. "Reforming," Merriam-Webster Dictionary, https://www.merriam-webster.com/dictionary/reforming.
4. Bell Textron, "Bell Intelligent Systems: An Innovation Journey with Microsoft Technology," February 11, 2021, https://news.bellflight.com/en-US/196184-bell-intelligent-systems-an-innovation-journey-with-microsoft-technology.
5. "Creation," Merriam-Webster Dictionary, https://www.merriam-webster.com/dictionary/creation.
6. J. Essinger, *Jacquard's Web: How a Hand-Loom Led to the Birth of the Information Age* (Oxford, UK: Oxford University Press, 2007).
7. Dana Mayor, "Joseph Marie Jacquard—Complete Biography, History and Inventions," History-Computer, December 15, 2022, https://history-computer.com/joseph-marie-jacquard-complete-biography.

CHAPTER 2

What Does It Mean to Be Human in the Era of Artificial Intelligence?

A child may ask, "What is the world's story about?" And a grown man or woman may wonder, "What way will the world go? How does it end and, while we're at it, what's the story about?"

—JOHN STEINBECK, *EAST OF EDEN*

Since the beginning of human cognition, humankind's search for meaning has produced works of art and literature, breakthroughs in science and technology, and voyages across oceans and into outer space. This search for meaning is so fundamental to the human experience as to exist independent of Maslow's hierarchy of needs, as evidenced by cave paintings from the Paleolithic Period, the Pyramids of Giza, and Wolfgang Amadeus Mozart composing his Requiem on his deathbed.

Despite this search's antiquity and the many cultures and individuals who believe that the question of the meaning of humankind has been answered, no collective answer has been found or agreed to. Perhaps this is why scientific and technological advancements, in particular, recenter the human gaze on the age-old question: What does it mean to be human?

What does it mean to be human if the Earth is not the center of the universe? (1543)

if we can journey beneath the ocean? (1776)

if we travel to the moon and beyond? (1969)

if machines can beat us at chess? (1997)

if machines can create art? (2018)

if machines can write convincingly? (2022)

This is not a question asked at the natural history museum. The fact that the upper-body strength of a gorilla is six times that of an adult human or that whales have greater empathy centers in their brains does not raise an existential question for humankind.

Yet when a new technology is introduced, if it holds any correlation to what has previously been considered an exclusively human capability or skill, it is met with fear and/or skepticism. As if what it means to be human is a checklist.

When one closes one's eyes and ponders what it means to be human, what comes to mind might be a memory of running through a forest in the golden hour of the afternoon, jumping into a lake amidst the laughter of friends, or being sung to sleep by a loved one. These kind of experiential memories are building blocks of how we assign meaning to our lives, and, although they reflect what it means to be human, they do not define the human experience. In other words, if someone sang to their computer every night, the computer would not become more human because it experienced the same thing a human child does.

Society stands on the precipice of the next great era of transformation, fueled by technology that is more complex and powerful by several orders of magnitude than its precedents. Addressing the existential question of what it means to be human in this era will lay the foundation for culture, the future of which is intertwined with economic growth, both inside and outside of organizations. It will also create common language and focus for coalitions across public and private sectors, nonprofits, and academia to address society's fundamental challenges. Lastly, it will provide individuals with tools to find meaning and grounding in the human–machine paradigm and its impact to the future of work and, more importantly, individual purpose.

It is not within the scope of this book to present a definition of what it means to be human. Rather, this book will highlight the need for these discussions to take place, propose frameworks for clarifying the distinction between humans and machines, and provide parallel economic, strategic, and technological frameworks and principles to guide individuals and organizations into and through their Autonomous Transformation journeys. These frameworks can be leveraged at the whiteboard when building a technological road map, in the boardroom when discussing the transformation agenda, or in a café between sips of coffee.

These frameworks lay the foundation for creating a more human future, which requires a mutual understanding of what it means to be human and therefore what would contribute to a *more* human future.

The Pain of Uncertainty

In 2016, a group of researchers in London performed a study in which participants were presented with an image of a rock and asked to guess whether there was a snake underneath the rock. After their guess, the correct answer was displayed (either an image of a snake, or text that read "No snake"), and regardless of the accuracy of their guess, each time a snake was presented, the participant would receive a painful electric shock on the back of their left hand. Throughout the experiment, the researchers altered the likelihood that a snake would appear, and observed a link between a higher degree of uncertainty and acute stress responses. They concluded that stress responses are tuned to environmental uncertainty and had a direct impact on task performance.[1]

This is one of dozens of studies that have linked the experience of uncertainty to physiological impacts, ranging from registering in the brain as physical pain to decreased performance and the ability to learn.

In the context of the era of artificial intelligence, uncertainty bears a significant cost for society, for employees, and for leaders. Given its physiological implications and the impact on the ability to learn and perform, there is a strong business case for eliminating uncertainty within the organization, the ecosystem, and society.

In Microsoft's transformation that began in 2014 when Satya Nadella took over as chief executive officer, this paradigm was memorialized by a nontraditional human resources leader, Joe Whittinghill, who established the leadership principle "Create Clarity" to address the psychological drive for certainty, especially in times of change. Where certainty may not be possible, clarity is nevertheless possible, an example of which is encapsulated in one of Microsoft's leadership mantras: "Get bad news out fast."

In the era of artificial intelligence, if you are a manager or organizational leader and there is a possibility that your team members are experiencing uncertainty about the future of their livelihoods against the backdrop of technological upheaval, there are both economic and moral reasons to create and communicate clarity.

In the context of the broader market, this phenomenon can be observed in real time with the latest technologies at any given point. With each technological breakthrough, humans experience a cycle of existential reconciliation, navigating uncertainty for the social, economic, and experiential impacts of each new breakthrough.

This generates a fiscal opportunity that should be monitored closely, as the desire for certainty can lead to quick transactions or misplaced trust in advisors who, regardless of intentions, may not have the expertise to deliver on creating the needed certainty.

Leaders who approach each new technological breakthrough that reaches the public discourse with a focus on generating clarity for their stakeholders, organizations, and team members will realize an economic benefit and contribute to a healthy workplace in which team members can focus on doing their best work while continuing to learn and grow.

Capability

The first and most basic distinction between humans and machines is **capability**.

Watching machines at work in a manufacturing plant is an unforgettable experience. When they perform as designed, they move with speed and precision, at times lifting enormously heavy objects or cutting through material with blades or lasers. They perform these tasks tirelessly, only pausing to resolve errors, accommodate production schedule changes, or for fixes and upgrades.

In parallel, systems in the banking industry detect fraudulent credit card charges by wading through oceans of data in milliseconds, analyzing against an individual's spending pattern, location, recent charges, and a number of other parameters to determine whether a charge should be approved or declined.

In Figure 2.1, the capabilities in which a machine can be considered distinctly better than a human map to the two examples above. If humans were to create products in a manufacturing plant without machines, it would take significantly longer, leading to longer wait times and increased prices, with the potential of rendering the products economically unfeasible. Likewise, fraudulent credit card charges would require an unbelievable amount of human workers to analyze at the scale that machines are capable, and would inevitably take much longer.

There is a relatively little-known example of human ingenuity that involves a violinist and a potato chip manufacturer. During the manufacturing process, chips are dipped in grease, which lingers and must be significantly reduced before the chips can move into the next stage of the process. The manufacturer believed a better process could be developed than their existing approach, which was effectively to shake the chips so that grease would slide off. Finding the balance between maximum grease removal and breaking the fewest possible chips was an ongoing and costly challenge.

The chip manufacturer put out a request for proposals for solving this problem, and inevitably received myriad technology-based proposals to slightly improve the process. The winning proposal, however, came from a violinist who proposed finding the resonant frequency of the grease, and playing a sound at that frequency that would vibrate the grease and not the chip.[2]

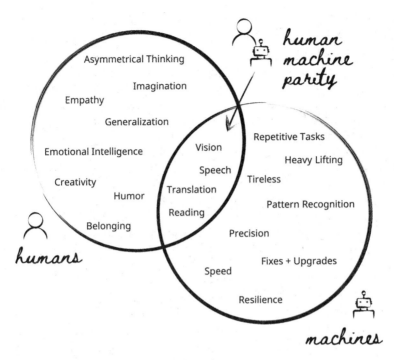

Figure 2.1   Capabilities of Humans and Machines

The approach was adopted, creating exponentially more value than the manufacturer had envisioned.

The ability to imagine and create is among the most fundamental of human characteristics. Artists across media, geographies, and throughout history have created renderings from the fantastic to the mundane that have directly and indirectly shaped cultures. This speaks to the left side of Figure 2.1, where empathy and asymmetrical thinking, for example, have been paired to imagine and create meaningful and impactful art.

For some readers this may bring generative artificial intelligence to mind, and DALL·E 2 and ChatGPT are great examples on which to practice this framework. For those who may not be familiar with DALL·E 2 and ChatGPT: DALL·E 2 renders images that have never existed but look like an artist or photographer created them, and ChatGPT writes text that is convincing enough for a reader to believe that a human could have written it.

At first glance, because each of these transformers can be focused on the subject of art, it might appear that machines have now developed the capability to imagine and create. At second glance, however, particularly at the technological underpinnings of these transformers, one can observe that they have been developed with unbelievably large sets of representative data and examples (DALL·E 2 consists of 3.5 billion parameters and GPT-3 consists of 175 billion parameters), the patterns of which are then leveraged to generate an image or a passage of text. Through the lens of the diagram in Figure 2.1, DALL·E and ChatGPT have reached new heights of elegance when it comes to the application of pattern recognition and speed, which falls squarely onto the right side of the diagram.

What would it look like for a machine to exhibit human-level creativity? It would need to move beyond *imitation* based on instructions or input (e.g., "A painting of a distinguished family of golden retrievers in the style of Rembrandt"[3]) to *creation*—bringing something original into existence through imaginative skill. As you read this, you are likely sitting amidst an overwhelming accumulation of applied human creativity. Maybe you are on a flight, hurtling through the air because the Wright Brothers invented a way to defy gravity. Perhaps you are nestled in an armchair by a fireplace because humans have innovated methods to tame fire and bring it into our homes for warmth and ambience. If you are reading this on a digital screen, there are not enough pages in this book to list the technological and scientific breakthroughs orchestrated to create what you are holding in your hands.

The role machines have played in all of this creation is remarkable utility in following instructions and extending human capability, both in the digital and physical spheres. The surface area to which human creativity can be applied has been expanded by several orders of magnitude thanks to machines.

An example of this in action is the development of a new product. A human applies empathy and imagination to imagine a new product. This product idea is then analyzed for viability. This involves steps such as determining whether there is a market for this new product, whether there are already competitors or preexisting patents, what it would cost to create the product, what could be charged for the product, whether there are channels for distribution, and so on. The application of machines in these analyses greatly expands the scope of research while simultaneously reducing the amount of time required. Throughout this analysis, the human is orchestrating several analytical methods across many different systems, all the while generalizing across these analysis points as answers are found—accruing to a mental model that ultimately determines whether the development of this new product is a worthwhile pursuit.

This is an example of the inherently complementary capabilities of humans and machines at their best. Humans can achieve more both by adding machine capabilities to their solution set as well as by offloading manual, repetitive tasks. This is possible because machines are capable of reaching parity with humans when it comes to perception tasks—vision, transcribing speech, translating, and reading.

Consciousness

The second distinction between humans and machines is **consciousness**. The first principle of the philosophy of René Descartes, a seventeenth-century French philosopher is "Cogito, ergo sum"—"I think, therefore I am." This is a critical distinction that remains intact as of this writing when it comes to humans and machines. There is not a machine in public existence that is conscious of itself from an existential perspective. That is a metaphysical phenomenon that has not been created and could not be achieved on accident (if at all).

As Edith Elkind, a computer science professor at the University of Oxford, put it, "Machines will become conscious when they start to set their own goals and act according to these goals rather than do what they were programmed to do. This is different from autonomy: Even a fully autonomous car would still drive from A to B as told."[4]

Machines do not possess the fundamental building blocks of the human psyche. They have no instinctive desires. This can be easy to forget for those familiar with branches of artificial intelligence, as negative and positive reinforcements are leveraged in reinforcement learning, but there has yet to be any indication that a machine craves positive reinforcement. They instead follow instructions, with positive and negative reinforcements indicating whether they are closer to completing the instruction and whether another attempt is required.

In 1980, John Searle, an American philosopher, created a thought experiment to demonstrate the narrowness (and therefore lack of consciousness) of machines that employ machine learning, called the Chinese Room Argument. It entails a person sitting alone in a room into which Chinese characters are slipped under the door. The person then follows instructions for which characters should be slipped back under the door in response, leading those outside the door to mistakenly believe that there is a Chinese speaker in the room. The takeaway from this thought experiment, simplified, is that the fact that a machine is able to translate Chinese into English does not mean that the machine understands either Chinese or English.

Consciousness is a more sensitive topic than capability, as it touches on a deeper question, particularly for those with a faith or religious background. The idea that machines could reach a point of consciousness at parity with humans can be interpreted to challenge the idea that the world was created by a higher power. It is important to be aware of this potential sensitivity when approaching this topic so as not to preclude the opportunity for meaningful and productive discussion.

It is worth noting here that leaders in technology and science have spoken publicly about concerns of the risk of machine consciousness. The risk machine consciousness would pose to humankind is inarguably high and unpredictable. However, the likelihood of machine consciousness being developed is a different story, as it lacks economic viability. Achieving this kind of technological breakthrough would likely require unbelievable amounts of data, the best and brightest minds from around the world, significant computing resources, and several preceding breakthroughs (such as quantum computing). At the end of that road of investment, there is little to no indication that profit would await the investing company or independent investor, and a high likelihood of existential risk. This, paired with the question as to whether it is even feasible in the first place, makes the development of machine consciousness unlikely in the present era.

Notes

1. A. O. de Berker, R. B. Rutledge, C. Mathys, L. Marshall, G. F. Cross, R. J. Dolan, and S. Bestmann, "Computations of Uncertainty Mediate Acute Stress Responses in Humans," *Nature Communications* 7 (March 29, 2016): 10996. doi:10.1038/ncomms10996.
2. Another interesting story on resonating frequencies: Nikola Tesla developed an earthquake machine leveraging the resonating frequency of the earth.
3. DALL·E 2's answer to this prompt can be found at brianevergreen.com/woofington
4. M. Weisberger, "Will AI Ever Become Conscious?," *LiveScience*, May 24, 2018, https://www.livescience.com/62656-when-will-ai-be-conscious.html (accessed January 15, 2023).

PART TWO
The Art of the Impossible

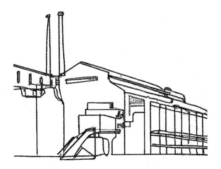

In the past the man has been first; in the future the system must be first.

—Frederick Winslow Taylor, *The Principles of Scientific Management*, 1911

CHAPTER 3

Our Inheritance

Humankind is facing some of the greatest existential and social challenges in history.

As science and technology have progressed, problems, or networks of problems, have become increasingly complex. The systems that make up our society have been scaffolded on top of other systems and are bending under the pressures of war, the climate crisis, child labor, racism, social divide, and the societal push to continuously build and stack more and more systems. In 2020, the word "systemic" leapt from the academic world to the international vernacular almost overnight, and no word better describes the interlocking nature of these challenges.

What does that have to do with artificial intelligence, the Internet of Things, digital twins/simulations, robotics, and mixed reality?

There has traditionally been an artificial divide between social systems and organizational systems. In the context of that divide, the development and application of these technologies within organizations would have nothing to do with social problems.

Fortunately or unfortunately, depending on your perspective, this divide has been shattered by the Information Age. People want to know where their food comes from, how their clothing is made, how energy is delivered to their homes, if their bank has bias in its loan application programs, and so on—and if they do not like the answer, they push for change through purchasing decisions, boycotts, strikes, and seeking policy change.

This means that initiatives within organizations that benefit the organization at the expense of society have become unviable. Initiatives that benefit the organization without consideration of societal impact are the most common, although they are decreasing, as organizations have begun building ethical practices into their rhythms of business. Initiatives that benefit the organization with a neutral societal impact are also common and neutrality is becoming a new standard. Then there are those who seek to use their influence and resources to create a positive societal impact.

I once met a vice president at one of the largest chocolate companies in the world who wanted to guarantee that there was no child labor in his company's supply chain.

He had considerable influence, was highly motivated, and was well positioned to take on this problem, or so it would seem.

If his company directly employed children, this problem would have been quickly solved by enforcing company policy, terminating those employees, and creating more governance to ensure it did not happen again.

Unfortunately, his situation was significantly more complicated. His company bought processed chocolate from a company that bought raw cacao from other companies that bought raw cacao from farmers. In other words, there were at least three layers between him and the farmers, and he had no information on the farmers or the companies that bought and aggregated the raw cacao from the farmers.

This was a systemic problem over which his organization, despite being an integral part of the system, could exercise no influence. The situation could be likened to a steering wheel, which, despite being a fundamental part within the system of an automobile and that which is closest to the customer (or driver), does not have the ability to fix a problem with the engine.

We met and discussed many ways that we might be able to resolve this challenge, such as creating a coalition of chocolate companies that may then be able to exercise influence over the companies that process their chocolate, which could then influence the companies that buy and aggregate raw cacao to share the list of farmers from whom they source chocolate. We discussed then using satellite imagery or drones to regularly inspect the farms, artificial intelligence to process the video data and identify any suspected child labor, blockchain to connect individual farms to batches of chocolate, and working with local government leaders for enforcement.

In other words, all of our ideas existed within the context of the system and were focused on either improving the system or adding new parts to the system. We were examining the situation through a mechanistic worldview.

Our Inheritance from the Industrial Revolution

There are countless examples like the above, where good intentions collide with systemic challenges and, despite alignment at the highest levels of the organization, strong ideas, and shared passion and momentum, the initiative does not move forward.

The issue lay not in the individual components, but in the process by which we endeavor to solve complex problems, which is incapable of producing the results we desire.

This is because these systems were built either within the context of the Industrial Revolution or on the foundation of systems built within the context of the Industrial Revolution.

Since the Industrial Revolution, organizations around the world have been incrementally improving and building on the original systems created during the Industrial Revolution with new mechanistic capabilities throughout the twentieth century, and with an overlay of digital capabilities in the era of Digital Reformation and Transformation.

This orientation is evident in the press and academic announcements around real-world applications of the next iteration of the Industrial Revolution (or Industry x.0). The Industrial Revolution broke work down to its most basic unit, referred to as a work element. In the ensuing era, all work elements that could be mechanized were mechanized, and all remaining work was assigned to human workers, in a move that treated workers like machines.

Subsequently, new machines were developed to take on additional tasks that had to be relegated to humans, which further devalued the human worker.

When digital capabilities were introduced to the market and what had been analog began to transition to digital wherever possible, more work could be done by the same number of people, but the relationship between humans and machines in the workplace remained the same.

At the organizational level, the systems designed in the Industrial Revolution, and their mechanistic worldview, remain intact, such as in organizational structures and in departments within universities. Generally speaking, students are aligned to a part of the system in which they are most interested in functioning. They then are instructed how best to operate as that part within a system, such as accounting, marketing, or engineering. Then, in most organizations around the world, graduates are hired into the functions for which they have been trained, and they serve as a functioning part of the broader system.

In other words, our organizations, companies, and governments have been developed from a mechanistic worldview—that is, as machines—based on the most advanced thinking of the Industrial Revolution. Since then, each generation has been charged with the maintenance and incremental improvement of those systems. This proceeding has met its logical end on two fronts.

First, incremental improvements cannot fundamentally change a system. This means that, despite the best intentions of individuals who would change the world, the existential and social challenges faced by our society today cannot be met by our existing systems and trajectory. To borrow from an earlier chapter, you cannot reform your way into a better future.

Second, the management and organizational systems of the Industrial Revolution are incompatible with the latest wave of technological advancements. This is evident in the statistics of how many machine learning models make it into production (13%) and how many businesses are reporting little to no return on investment for their initiatives focused on artificial intelligence, digital twins and simulations, the Internet of Things, robotics, and mixed reality.

Taylorism, or Scientific Management

Taylorism, named after its inventor, Frederick Winslow Taylor, is predicated on the idea that there is one "best" way to do any task, and that by analysis—breaking the task into smaller, simpler parts and studying each part separately—we can find the most efficient and productive way to perform the task as a whole. It was a revolutionary approach to management that transformed the way factories were run in the early twentieth century.

This was not just about increasing efficiency and productivity; it was about a fundamental shift in the way people thought about work. It was about the belief that the best way to improve the performance of any worker was to study their every move and find ways to make them do their job faster and better. It was about the idea that there was always a better way to do things, and that the best way was the one that required the least amount of effort. This shift in thinking was groundbreaking at the time, applying the scientific method to management (hence its other name, scientific management).

But as we delve deeper, we begin to see the hidden costs of Taylorism. The application of Taylorism in the workplace led to a dehumanization of work, treating workers as cogs in a machine and taking away their autonomy.

Taylorism also led to the systematic removal of creativity and spontaneity, as every task is standardized, and there is no room for improvement or experimentation. Tasks were defined by "experts" and executed by workers.[1]

Throughout the twentieth century, Taylorism continued to change the way people thought about work and efficiency, and laid the foundation for other disciplines that apply the scientific method, continuing to shape the way people view the worker and their role in the workplace.

A short list of examples of tools that Taylorism contributed to management thinking illustrates its pervasiveness in corporate culture even today: process analysis, process mapping, elimination of waste, process optimization, knowledge transfer, measures of efficiency, process documentation, and best practices.

The application of the scientific method to our thinking processes has become so pervasive that it influences how organizations brainstorm, the criteria by which ideas are selected, the design of experiments, and measurements of effectiveness—it is comfortable because it is objective and abdicates risk.

The scientific method is dangerous when it leads to a focus on measurement over impact, particularly within an organization that operates mechanistically, as individual parts within a larger machine.

This can be observed in a standard monthly business review, filled with summarized metrics, in which each team is achieving its goals disconnected from the performance of the overall organization. If the marketing team has satisfied its quota for lead generation and the total number of impressions and engagement is higher than ever, and the sales team has had a record quarter, closing more deals than ever before, and the engineering team has increased product quality and output over last quarter while lowering cost, who is accountable for the fact that customers are choosing a competitor's product?

Pause and consider what your mind did with that question. Did you think of the other organizations that could have been involved? Maybe checking customer service metrics would reveal that customers are frustrated with our customer service process. It could also be a design problem, but then again the designers met the design specifications on time and under budget.

In other words, analysis has become an automatic response to most questions—taking the system apart and looking for objective data from which to understand a larger problem. And this *is* an important method by which to explain what is going on within a system. But it cannot explain *why*. Analysis provides explanation, but not understanding.

Diagnostic analytics is the combination of analysis and synthesis to provide understanding and answer the question of *why*: analysis to understand what happened and where it happened (production has slowed in factory *x*), synthesis to examine the larger context and form hypotheses (have there been any changes in management or process in factory *x*?), analysis to test those hypotheses—cycling through this process until an answer is found. In the context of analytics and data science, analysis falls within the expertise of the data scientist or machine learning engineer. Synthesis in this context requires an understanding of the domain, which therefore requires the domain expert. There are many organizations that have found that balance within diagnostic analytics through persistent trial and error, but it should be noted that the formal definitions of diagnostic analytics from credible and widely acknowledged resources do not include synthesis, and explanations of the process only mention the need for technical resources.

This is one of the contributing factors to the failure of artificial intelligence and emerging technological initiatives. Leaders and managers seeking to better understand the performance of their companies have been excited by the ability for machine learning to process more data and faster than a human could, and thereby glean insights into how the company could better perform. Unfortunately, by nature of the fact that machine learning is an analysis tool, while it can be leveraged to explain what is happening in the organization, it cannot explain why. Additionally, predictive and prescriptive analytics, both of which are phenomenal capabilities within the proper contexts, are easy to misinterpret based on their naming conventions. Predictive analytics is a perfect tool for applying the scientific method to a business process: Based on what has happened, if the context stays the same, what will happen again? Prescriptive analytics takes this a step further by combining predictions with business rules: Based on what has happened, if the context stays the same, what should be done when it happens again?

There have been many notable examples of the proper implementation of these technologies, but organizations that have invested in initiatives seeking to implement predictive and prescriptive analytics within their organizations to identify and understand things that their own experts do not understand about what will happen or what to do in the future are exemplifying the art of the impossible and designing for failure. This experience has produced many leaders who consider themselves to have tried artificial intelligence and now believe it to just be hype or that the technology is not quite where it needs to be to be useful or practical.

Data Science Taylorism*

The principle process by which Taylorism was applied to increase effectiveness in the twentieth century was through careful observation by an external expert holding a stopwatch, meticulously documenting, timing, and applying the scientific method to analyze workers' production processes. These external experts then produced an optimized design for each individual task, a process by which the skills to complete those tasks could best be learned, and a proposed schedule for each individual worker with a targeted threshold of quality and output.

Unfortunately, this is almost indistinguishable from the principle process by which many consulting and technology firms have approached the application of data science for their customers and clients.

In Taylorism, scientific management experts collaborated with managers in order to improve the work of the "man of sluggish type, [. . .] an educated mechanic, or even an intelligent laborer."[2]

---

* Data Science Taylorism is distinct from "Digital Taylorism" or "New Taylorism," which has been defined as the use of monitoring technology to apply a form of scientific management at scale, where the scientific management expert with the stopwatch has been replaced by cameras, sensors, and automated data analysis.

In Data Science Taylorism, data science experts collaborate with managers with the aim of gleaning answers in the data to then educate or better assign tasks to the engineers and front-line workers. This approach dismisses the expertise of those closest to the customers and processes in favor of data.

I have observed well-meaning individuals attempt to follow this process in hopes of achieving value on behalf of customers and clients, but this approach increases the social divide between technologists and domain experts (more on that in Chapter 13), drastically reduces the likelihood of project success, and can be credited for a healthy portion of the 87% of machine learning models that never make it into production.

Notes

1. Pierre Bourdieu, *The Social Structures of the Economy* (Polity Press, 2005).
2. F. W. Taylor, the story of Schmidt, from Chapter 2 of *Principles of Scientific Management* (1910).

CHAPTER 4

Maintenance Mode

When I met with leaders from one of the largest public utilities companies in the world for an artificial intelligence strategy summit, one of the questions posed to me and my team was our position on deregulation in the utilities sector, that is, allowing more competition into the market and enabling customers to invest in generating their own electricity, removing their reliance on the power grid. The deregulation movement began in the 1970s and as of 2018, 17 of the states in the United States have passed a form of deregulation into law.[1]

I probed for the rationale behind the question and learned that they preferred to partner with those who were not in favor of deregulation, as it threatened their revenue and market leadership position.

My next question was whether they were investing in self-generation systems and solutions so that they would be positioned to become the global leader if and when deregulation took place. I posited that if they were to develop and test such a product within markets and states that are not regulated, it could create a global revenue stream outside of their regulated footprint, providing ample testing ground to prove and refine the product.

This was not something they had considered. Rather than invest in the possibility of being a global leader in self-generation of power, they were focused on ensuring that a change in the regulatory landscape did not take place, as it would present an existential threat to their organization. This is because they were focused on maintaining the existing system.

Centuries-Old Systems

In the process of manufacturing, which could be considered the beating heart of the Industrial Revolution, a single anomaly can create a disaster. It might be something entering a machine that does not belong that could cause a machine to break down or threaten the safety of those working near the machine, or a slight damage to a component of a machine that, unchecked, produces hundreds of flawed products that need to be scrapped. There are both physical and fiscal reasons to streamline anything that can possibly be streamlined to avoid an anomaly.

Throughout our contemporary systems lay evidence that the Industrial Revolution effectively built the backbone of society in the late nineteenth century and throughout the twentieth century, evangelizing the effectiveness of streamlining and the evils of anomalies. Schools that have been standardized to one form of learning, standardized tests to measure intelligence or knowledge, standard operating procedures across industries, even the eight-hour workday and the concept of a weekend away from work were invented during this era (the last two thanks to Henry Ford). In the contemporary era, it is difficult to pass a single hour of time without interacting with centuries-old systems.

These systems were built on the foundation of viewing the world as a machine, each piece a subsystem of the bigger machine. The fallout of this worldview is that it requires people to operate as if they are components within a broader machine, leading them to feel like cogs.

As it stands in the early twenty-first century, the world has been architected, with few exceptions, within the context of this mechanistic worldview. Whether an organization was built 100 years ago to create a new system or 30 years ago to reinforce a system, many organizations find themselves in an endless cycle of making improvements (reformation) but very few reimagine the original design. This is a natural outcome of the life cycle of organizations.

The majority of systems naturally reach a developmental stage where internal and external factors begin to pressure the system to maintain stability, and only change in small increments. This leads organizations to become trapped by the reliance their customers have built on their products and price points, forcing them into "maintenance mode."

Maintenance mode is an organizational state in which preservation and incremental improvement become the central orientation of the organization.

There are three telltale signs by which an organization can be assessed for maintenance mode:

1. Criteria for initiatives across the organization include an orientation toward making incremental improvements without disrupting the system.
2. Approved initiatives improve individual functions without impacting broader organizational performance.
3. Organizational risk tolerance is extremely low, often indicated by a rigid return on investment justification requirement.

Directly following the release of a product or service and broad market adoption, signs 1 and 3 would be important indicators of long-term continuity of the product or service. The same is true for operational leaders who need to maintain continuity of the organization's core value proposition. These are ideal arenas for reformation; although transformation can and does apply to these organizations, the allowable risk tolerance is often better suited to reformational initiatives.

Where maintenance mode becomes a problem is its prevalence in an organizational culture across all functions and at all levels, and it is a natural outcome of much of the most popular management thinking and leadership frameworks of the twentieth century and early twenty-first century.

Maintenance Mode as a Means of Sustaining Scaffolded Systems

Scaffolded systems are the most challenging to change. The scaffolding of systems that comprise the utilities sector, for example, contains a subsystem of power generation, which contains further subsystems of coal refineries, nuclear generators, solar farms, and wind farms. The utilities sector also contains a subsystem called the energy grid, which, oversimplified, delivers energy to everything from streetlamps to skyscrapers within its geography. The utilities sector, examined as a part of the larger system of society, serves the critical function of supporting medical facilities, data centers, computers, and communication networks. A deeper layer to this complexity is that utilities, in developed countries, is a heavily regulated sector, meaning there are legal policies in place governing activities such as how utilities organizations spend their money, how they communicate with their customers, and where and how they store their data.

As you can imagine, introducing a change to this scaffolding of systems is difficult not only from a complexity point of view, but also from the vertical scaffolding point of view, in that the implications in the case of a system failure are disastrous.

Within the context of a scaffolding of systems such as these, investment in initiatives focused on emerging technologies is understandably met with systemic resistance.

If a new island with a landmass equal to the size of Europe appeared in the Pacific Ocean and its utilities sector could be designed from the beginning (as an act of creation), with all the technologies currently available and without existing utilities systems in place to maintain and keep it stable, it would undoubtedly be the most advanced utilities system on the planet. The path from an existing system to a more advanced system or set of scaffolded systems, however, is much more challenging and counterintuitive than the incremental, return on investment–based accounting in place within the majority of organizations today.

Each industry vertical is an interconnected network of scaffolded systems that faces three primary impediments to system-wide change.

First, the complexity of scaffolded systems makes the consideration of change an exercise that involves a higher degree of complexity, vulnerability, and risk than any other business activity in empathy, research, ideation, analysis and synthesis, prototyping, testing, partnership, negotiation, leadership, and so on.

Second, in most organizations, no one below the executive office is accountable, in terms of measures tied to incentives, for improving the performance of the system as a whole or for improving the interaction of their part of the system with the rest of the system. The leaders of each part are incented and relied on to ensure that their part of the system continues to operate smoothly and at the highest possible performance. At its worst, when an initiative fails or organizational performance degrades, this orientation passes the blame from part to part, or team to team, when the failure is actually a product of the interactions within the whole system and not an individual part or team.

Third, accounting systems within organizations account for actions and risks taken and whether or not they were successful, but not for actions and risks that were not taken and whether or not they would have been successful.

Maintenance Mode and Advanced Technologies

Against this backdrop, there is an indication as to why there has been little meaningful adoption of artificial intelligence and other emergent technologies. Organizations in maintenance mode naturally reject anything that would introduce a system-wide change and therefore threaten the stability of the system on which its customers rely. Pressured by shareholders, leaders, or customers, these organizations have a natural tendency to explore emergent technological advancements through pilots, a situation in which rigorous justification of the pilot was not required, and therefore there is no path to production. For many years, technology and advisory firms engaged happily in pilots, often offering investment eager to demonstrate their capabilities. In more recent years, however, as pilot after pilot has failed to convert to a larger partnership regardless of its ability to achieve the goal of the pilot, this model has begun to be called into question by technology leaders. This prevalent phenomenon has been termed "pilot purgatory."

Other organizations in maintenance mode have responded to these technologies by hiring or promoting a leader to build a team or capability around these technologies and partner with the rest of the organization to identify, design, and execute initiatives to achieve efficiencies. For many organizations, this model has yielded better results than the pilot purgatory model, but not without significant investment and internal resistance. Given the small number of data and decision scientists in the market, combined with organizational leaders who may not have the expertise to accurately assess the trustworthiness and credibility of these experts, many of these budding teams spend years researching without a clear path to implementation or return on investment and are subsequently shut down or face shuffles of leadership in hopes of achieving the right organizational formula to generate practical value.

This is further complicated by a lack of practical experience and the orientation of many who go into the field of data science, who are trained and recognized for seeking breakthrough applications to extend the scientific field, leading to patents, research papers, and awards. If data scientists are particularly enterprising and emerge with a doctor of philosophy (PhD) at the age of 25 and enter the market, they have approximately 40 working years, or 80 projects (given a generous assumption of only six months per project throughout their career) in which to leave their mark on the world of science and academia. This context, combined with the scarcity of data scientists and the resultant supply of high-paying options, renders it difficult to hire, train, and retain data scientists to solve known or mundane organizational needs, regardless of their monetary value. The organizational desire to leverage data science, which remains a nascent field, to make low-risk, incremental improvements to the system is at odds with the interests and intrinsic motivation of many data scientists.

An analogous equivalent to this dilemma would be if corporations were to hire budding astronauts and ground them, as space presents too much risk, and instead wanted them to recreate research findings achieved by other astronauts who did go to space, translating their findings into projects specific to their organization to achieve a decrease in cost or increase in profit.

Maintenance mode is at odds with exploration, and organizations in maintenance mode that endeavor, with the best of intentions and even with significant investment, will struggle to harness the potential of artificial intelligence and its adjacent technologies.

Is Technology the Problem or the Solution?

The lack of successful implementations of advanced technologies has led to a self-reinforcing cycle of negative outcomes, leading to increasing skepticism and the assignment of blame on the technology or on those implementing the technology. This is difficult to ratify with the incredible feats technology organizations have been able to achieve, subsequently making up 7 of the

10 most valuable public companies in the world at the time of this writing, and five of the seven companies in the world whose market capitalizations have, at any point, exceeded $1 trillion.

The technology is neither the problem nor the solution alone. Technology organizations that have leveraged advanced technologies within the context of acts of creation in the market have transformed markets and achieved new heights of value creation. In contrast, technology organizations, arguably with the same degree of talent and, in many cases, more assets at the onset, that have not performed acts of creation or transformation in recent history but have been stuck in maintenance mode, have not been able to grow by the same order of magnitude as technology organizations that either created from nothing (such as Google, Netflix, and Amazon), or managed to overcome maintenance mode and perform acts of creation and transformation (such as Apple and Microsoft).

Even at the executive level, there can be a disconnect between incentives and accountability tied to system maintenance as opposed to acts of creation and transformation. In publicly traded companies, for example, a large portion of executive incentives are made up of shares of the corporation, the value of which is not tied to the performance of the system in its function as a part of a larger system, but to the perception of shareholders, largely based on sustained growth. Acts of creation, which require strategic, multiyear investment, can negatively impact financial performance of the organization in the short term, leading to decreased shareholder confidence and a decrease in pay for the leadership team and any employees participating in profit-sharing or stock option programs. Maintenance mode, although unsustainable in the long term, is profitable in the short term.

This prevalence of maintenance mode and its related metrics can be observed in the naming convention of the event that takes place each quarter that has the biggest consistent impact on stock trajectory: the earnings call. It is not a performance call, although the terms are often used interchangeably. It is also not a strategy call. If the function of an organization in a given subsection of the market is to provide necessary goods for the home at an affordable price, and the leadership announced that, in a given quarter, they had managed to improve the system so much that they could drastically reduce prices and maintain the same profit margin, the performance of the company in its essential function within society would have been improved, but unfortunately, shareholder confidence in the leadership team would likely decline along with its stock performance.

It is exceedingly difficult to introduce system-wide change from within a system. Out of the five well-known, system-wide changes in the following table, only one of them was introduced from within the system. American Airlines introduced a technology in 1978 to enable travel agents to make reservations using an online system, which was ultimately leveraged to create

Travelocity 18 years later. Otherwise, the system-wide changes, often despite the fact that the change was initially conceived from within a market leader within that industry vertical (such as within Kodak and Blockbuster), were introduced from outside these organizations—not because these organizations tried and failed, either. The conception never gained enough internal traction within the large organizations to create a new line of business or introduce a product or service that could disrupt the whole system.

Industry	System-Wide Change	Year of Introduction	Company	Inside or Outside?
Photography	Digital film	1990	Dycam Founded in 1988	Outside (first prototype created by an employee of Kodak in 1975)
Books	Online bookstore	1995	Amazon Founded in 1994	Outside (Borders outsourced online sales to Amazon, B&N.com launched in 1997)
Travel	Online travel agency	1996	Travelocity Founded in 1996	Inside (based on technology developed in 1978 by American Airlines)
Healthcare	Telemedicine	2005	Teledoc Founded in 2002	Outside
Entertainment	Streaming	2007	Netflix Founded in 1997	Outside (Blockbuster on Demand piloted in 1995, more in Chapter 17)

The Coexistence of Maintenance and Creation

The process of overcoming maintenance mode is not a cross-organizational pivot away from maintaining the systems on which customers rely to the act of creating new products and services in the marketplace. Rather, some resources should be devoted to maintaining system stability while other resources pivot to creating a vision for the future of the organization within society, the market, and its place in time. This vision should not take into account the current system during the vision-setting phase. Rather than beginning the process with the question "Where do we go from here?," the process should begin with "What ought to be?"

Answering the question of "Where do we go from here?" can lead to fine-tuning ships and inventing new tools for whaling in 1890, more aerodynamic carriages in 1908, or analyzing video footage of Blockbuster stores to create heat maps of foot traffic in 2007.

Once the question of "What ought to be?" is answered, the next question is "How do we get there from here?"

This process will be discussed further throughout this book.

A Note for Individual Contributors

One of the most impactful conversations I had during my tenure at Microsoft was with my former boss, Jennifer Byrne, when she was the chief technology officer for Microsoft US. I was expressing frustration over the metrics that had been tied to a portion of the budget our team had received from another team, as I felt that achieving those metrics would require operational focus on those numbers disconnected from and even opposed to the potential for market impact that had attracted me to the position.

"Screw the metrics," she told me.

She went on to ask me what market impact had attracted me to the position, and what I wanted to achieve within the next year. ("What ought to be?")

I answered her question, and she asked me: "If you achieved those things, wouldn't you blow the metrics out of the water?"

Even in a position where I did not have full control over all the metrics assigned to me or tied to budgetary allocation, this pivot enabled me to focus on the impact I wanted to have and see the metrics as milestones on that journey, as opposed to chasing the metrics for metrics' sake, which could have been achieved without creating lasting market impact.

The same holds true in an individual contributor position: if you do not have control over your metrics, the first step is to imagine the market impact you would like to create, and see the metrics as milestones on that journey. If the market impact you imagine is incompatible with the metrics you have been assigned, you can summarize the market impact you would like to achieve together with proposed new metrics, and if that does not work, it might not be possible to create the market impact you want to create at this stage in your career within the system you are in, and it might be time to look for your next adventure either internal or external to the organization.

Note

1. "Retail Electric Rates in Deregulated and Regulated States: 2018 Update," American Public Power Association, April 2019, https://www.publicpower.org/system/files/documents/2019%282018 data%29 Retail Electric Rates_final.pdf.

PART THREE
Envision Your Future

Leading people requires not only sensing change afoot, but imagining a brighter future and communicating it in a way that motivates others to follow you there.

—Nancy Duarte

CHAPTER 5

Requiem for the Industrial Revolution: Rehumanizing Work

I n the world of classical music, epochs have built upon the work of one another. Melodies, progressions, rhythms, instruments, vocal and instrumental pedagogy—they have evolved and been passed down from generation to generation through written, performed, and, more recently, recorded tradition. Arguably, the epoch of classical music that has left the most far-reaching impression on the way we experience music is the Romantic era, in which performers first began to interpret music through their own emotional connection to the notes and melodies, accelerating or decelerating as best fit their interpretation.

This paradigm shift is so embedded in the way humans experience music in the post-Romantic era that musicians from all over the world have recast music from epochs that predate the Romantic era, such as the Renaissance, Baroque, and Classical eras, through the Romantic lens of interpretation. Musical purists find this phenomenon frustrating, because they would prefer to hear Baroque music, for example, as it was intended and would have been played at that time, following a consistent tempo, celebrating precision, with no concept of speeding up or slowing down individual passages.

Another example of the Romantic era's impact on society and even our mental constructs regarding art and music is the elevation of the artist. Before the Romantic era, being a classical composer in Europe was a trade, having evolved from the time of the bards, cultural ceremonial music, and music in the context of the church to a modest, but funded, position in service of the church, a noble, or a royal benefactor. Johann Sebastian Bach, one of the most famous names in the history of music, did not become wealthy from the more than 11,000 compositions he produced in his lifetime. His varied use of instruments within his compositions was not the product of genius, but of the farmers who made it to rehearsal any given week and committed to be at the church that weekend, and the instruments they played. Rather, his genius lay in his endless ability to compose beautiful, cohesive works of music incorporating varied instrumentation in a short period of time.

The Romantic era changed this paradigm for all artists, represented famously in a letter Beethoven left behind when he broke ties with a former benefactor: "Prince, what you are, you are through chance and birth; what I am, I am through my own labor. There are many princes and there will continue to be thousands more, but there is only one Beethoven."[1]

The aftereffects of this shift in worldview are so prevalent that they would be difficult to unwind. Deconstructing the concept of artists back into a pre-Romantic view would mean a context in which painters have no prospect of achieving wealth, but can make a modest living by painting portraits and commissions for the wealthy, poets write love sonnets for the wealthy, composers set them to music, and so on. Each returns to their humble home at the end of a long day (that is, if they do not live at the home of the noble or royal together with their family) where their craft has yielded just enough wages to put food on the table, much like the rest of the hired staff of a given estate. This would be as if Sir Paul McCartney lived at Buckingham Palace, solely performed for the royal family and their guests, and did not make enough wages to rent his own flat.

This is the magnitude of the mindset shift required of leaders in the twenty-first century. The Industrial Revolution has been deeply threaded into the way we think about, talk about, approach, and manage organizations, initiatives, teams, and systems.

The evolutionary trajectory of the Industrial Revolution has met its logical resting place (*requiem* is Latin for "rest," and the name of the Catholic Mass for the laying of souls to rest in the context of a funeral). Those who endeavor to lead the ongoing progression of societal growth are coining new cycles of the Industrial Revolution (e.g., Industry *x*.0), but what they are describing, even in Industry 4.0, while a strong vision for the future of organizations, has not and will not transform society to the degree envisioned, much less create a more human future, through the vehicle of the Industrial Revolution.

The time has come to break out of the local minutiae of the Industrial Revolution. It is time for a decisive, worldwide shift toward a new way of thinking about, talking about, approaching, and managing organizations, initiatives, teams, and systems.

Artificial intelligence and its adjacent technologies highlight the need for a new way of thinking and working as well as create an opportunity to extend human capability and positively change the nature of work.

In 1911, Frederick Taylor, the creator of Scientific Management, and a key influencer of management thinking throughout the twentieth century and the early twenty-first century, said, "In the past the man has been first; in the future the system must be first."

Over 100 years later, we are a new breed of humanity, armed with knowledge of the entire world at our fingertips, wisdom handed down through the invention of video and audio recording combined with increased longevity, and we walk around with more power in our pockets and on our wrists than it took to send the first humans to the moon.

Whether you are a member of the executive leadership team of an organization, a manager, an individual contributor, a researcher, or a student, if you believe that we can do better—that we can create a more human future—the rest of this book will walk you through a set of tools and frameworks for beginning to disentangle from the Industrial Revolution, as well as a path forward in the direction of a more human future built on the foundation of Profitable Good.

Note

1. Rick Fulker, "Why Beethoven Snubbed Princes and Put His Music First," DW, September 12, 2016, https://www.dw.com/en/why-beethoven-snubbed-princes-and-put-his-music-first/a-19544501.

CHAPTER 6

The Problem with Solving Problems: Introducing Future Solving

I f you were to write down the three most innovative creations from your career or from your organization, what would they be, and when were they invented?

In the life cycle of an organization, once an innovative breakthrough is made and a system is developed, leaders of each individual part of the system are incented to optimize their individual parts. This is aligned with organizational structures as well as the educational system, and is an inheritance of the Industrial Revolution and mechanistic thinking. If an organization is a large machine, then the individual parts should be designed to run smoothly, improve incrementally, and reduce risk.

In 1951, a leader at Bell Labs called a meeting of departmental leaders and entered the room in a charged emotional state. He grimly announced that the telephone system of the United States had been destroyed the preceding night. The leaders were confused, as many had used the telephone that morning. He proceeded to restate that the telephone system had been destroyed and that anyone who did not believe so by noon that day would be terminated. He had their attention.

After a sufficient amount of pause and allowing the leaders to process his assertion and threat, he began to laugh and released the tension. By manner of explanation, he asked the room about the most meaningful contributions to the development of telephonic communications ever made by Bell Labs, which had recently been recognized in an article in *Scientific American* as the best group of industrially based laboratories in the world.

The answers were unanimous:

- The dial, which was introduced in the 1930s, but invented in the late 1800s.
- The ability to transmit multiple conversations simultaneously over one wire, which was introduced between the world wars, but invented in the late 1800s.
- The coaxial cable that connected the United States and Great Britain, which was built in 1882.

"Doesn't it strike you as odd," he said, "that the three most important contributions this laboratory has ever made to telephonic communications were made before any of you were born? What in the world have you been doing?" he asked. "I'll tell you," he said. "You have been improving the parts of the system taken separately, but you have not significantly improved the system as a whole."

"The deficiency," he said, "is not yours, but mine. We've had the wrong research and development strategy. We've been focusing on improving parts of the system rather than focusing on the system as a whole. [...] We have to restart by focusing on designing the whole and then designing parts that fit it rather than vice versa. Therefore, we are going to begin by designing the system with which we would replace the existing system right now if we were free to replace it with whatever system we wanted."

What ensued was an influx of inventions, including some well-known inventions ubiquitous in the late twentieth century, such as the touch-tone phone and caller identification.[1]

Nearly every organizational leader with whom I have discussed innovation wants to be an innovative leader. When that leader stands before a whiteboard, however, it is extremely rare for a leader, steeped in their organizational, industrial, market, and societal context, to propose an idea that does not focus on an individual part of the system.

Ironically, the inability to think systemically is a systemic problem. In the majority of cases, incentives, training, and experiences have groomed leaders and managers to drive and report short, incremental improvements on the existing system.

I was once brought in to advise one of the top telecommunications companies on a challenge they were facing related to their technology strategy. Their business-critical, monolithic applications were running on servers for which support was ending in approximately 10 months. Their strategy was focused on updating the applications as needed to migrate to the next set of on-premise servers, and I was asked to weigh in on nuances regarding the technology and the viability of their strategy. From a systems perspective, they were hoping to replace a part and slightly improve the performance of the part without disrupting the system.

I asked if they had considered migrating to the cloud, and was informed that, although migrating to the cloud was their long-term plan, it was not possible to rearchitect the monolithic applications into microservices, develop those microservices, and deploy to the cloud before support would end for the existing servers.

After some digging, it turned out that an offhand comment from one of the leaders of the initiative about how it would take too long to rearchitect the applications was the foundation for eliminating the consideration of migrating to the cloud, and no one had spoken with the development team.

I spoke with the development team, who had been hoping for the opportunity to eliminate technical debt by rearchitecting and rebuilding the applications, and they were confident it could be done. The team rallied, built momentum, generated their case, and presented to the executives, who accepted their proposal. Within the next 10 months, they achieved their goal and significantly improved the performance and capability of the system.

This is an example of the value that can be created when the orientation of investment and effort moves away from solving problems and toward designing and building an envisioned future.

Problem Solving versus Future Solving

The rhetoric of problem solving is pervasive in contemporary discourse. Leaders across sectors, ironically, in trying to solve the problem of leading with technology instead of outcomes, are quoted in books and articles, refocusing the conversation on "what problems need to be solved."

In an interview for this book, an esteemed academic leader told me that "the largest gap is connecting a problem a company wants to solve with the technology that's available."

But the problem with solving problems is that solving a problem is inherently directed at that which you do not want, not at what you *do* want.

As demonstrated in Figure 6.1, the problem-solving process begins at the starting point with the question: "What problems do we need to solve?"

The answer to that question is infinity. Organizations face an infinite number of problems at any given moment. The first step of narrowing the infinite number of problems is often to list the most top-of-mind problems, then socialize the list with others in the organization. Once the list has made a couple of revisionary rounds, an algebraic formula for determining which problem(s) to start with is developed. An example of this would be the

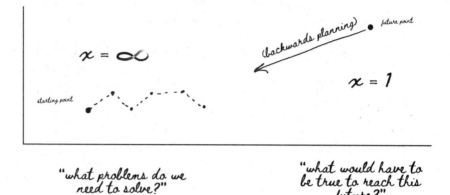

PROBLEM SOLVING   FUTURE SOLVING

Figure 6.1   Problem Solving and Future Solving

projected benefit of solving the problem, paired with the cost of implementation and length of time. A subset of problems are chosen, and the solving process begins.

During this process, the organization is backing into the future, as it is not aimed at a specific future. The organization is instead aimed at each problem that is closest to it and the most painful at any given time.

If I asked you to get into a time machine and go into a future scenario with me, would it matter which coordinates were programmed into the machine?

Future solving presents a new encapsulation of preexisting but underutilized methods, distinct from problem solving, by which organizational leaders and managers can advance into the future with clarity of direction.

The first question posed in future solving is "What ought to be?"

The second question, looking backwards from the envisioned future point to the starting point, is "What would have to be true to reach this future?"

This is a much simpler process, as it reduces the number of possibilities from infinite to one. The question of what would have to be true to reach this future can be recursively asked, building a path backwards until there is a clear path from the starting point to the envisioned future point, which could consist of a string of digital and autonomous reformation and transformation initiatives together with acts of creation.

When I first met with a contracts team at one of the top technology companies in the world, they had undergone a series of problem-solving steps, and had arrived at an undesirable future.

Their process began with the need to determine how to handle digital contracts signed through an electronic signing services platform since their process was based on written contracts. They resolved this problem by creating a shared email inbox to which all the emails from the electronic signing services platform would be directed. The next problem was to create and maintain a list of all of the existing contracts, which used to be manually entered into a spreadsheet when signed contracts arrived in the mail. They had resolved this through developing a process by which various team members would monitor, flag, and check off emails as they typed the contract information into a shared spreadsheet and saved the attached document into a shared folder.

The next problem presented to the team was the need to analyze the information in the spreadsheet and create graphs without risking any data integrity issues or loss. They resolved this by copy-pasting the data for the relevant time period (based on regular reports and point-in-time stakeholder requests) into a different spreadsheet that was preloaded with a variety of formulas to accelerate the analytical process.

The next problem was presentation, as their leadership was not interested in screenshots from the spreadsheet or in opening an attached spreadsheet, so they created a Word document template into which they would copy-paste the graphs and export to a PDF file. They then attached this file to an email template, updated the template, and hit send.

The final problems they faced, which led to calling my team in to help, was how slowly the spreadsheet software ran due to the number of rows and columns, as well as the risk of anything happening to the data.

For context, the market capitalization of this technology organization was over $400 billion at this time. They had the technological prowess and the resources to create a better solution, but the process by which they solved individual problems in succession led to a highly inefficient, risky position.

The question posed to me and my team was if we could improve the performance of the spreadsheet despite the large amounts of data; that is, "This problem needs to be solved."

Bear in mind that these were remarkably intelligent business leaders and managers at one of the most successful organizations in the world, following the prevailing management philosophy of doing the work that needs to be done with a bias for action and for solving problems as they present themselves to achieve efficiencies.

The process we followed as we scoped a potential partnership and engagement began with the question of what would have to be true for this process to be equally or more dependable without any step of the process requiring manual intervention.

For that to be true, there would need to be a way to either scrape the attachments of the emails as they came in to extract the necessary data, or the electronic signing services platform would need to have a means of sending us data each time a contract was fully executed alongside the email. Fortunately, they had the capability to do precisely that (through their Application Programming Interface or API)—send the data and the PDF that could be handled programmatically (i.e., by our software application)—and we were able to automate the first step of the team's process by building that integration, creating a database in which to store the data, and a folder in which to store the files.

For each subsequent step, we asked what would have to be true in order for no manual intervention to be required, and the final product was a software application that interacted directly with the electronic signing services platform and other internal systems, automatically generated the graphs the team used to create in a spreadsheet, with the addition of new graphs and a series of filters, which meant that the team no longer needed to create the regularly scheduled reports, most of the point-in-time reports could be self-serve directly in the tool, and the data could be exported for further analysis when needed.

This paved the way for improving this team's performance in its core function as well as transforming its interaction with other teams that relied on their information and their ability to advise on, build, and execute contracts.

Had we begun with the problem statement presented to us, we might have built a new spreadsheet software capable of processing more rows or proposed that they migrate to a different platform that would serve the same function within their process without reimagining their process.

The Use Case Problem

The field of agriculture is an exciting frontier for the application of technology. The developments in intelligence that can be distributed to edge systems enable solutions that can span the acreage of a farm or a collection of farms at a cost-effective price point.

Agricultural science (or agriscience) organizations have invested heavily in technologies such as remote sensing, the analysis of satellite imagery, developing drones, machine learning, and robotics. A notable example of the subsequent advancement of scientific research through technology is the ability to correctly identify leaf damage from a fungal pathogen from drone imagery.

The typical path to determine investment across industries, not just agriscience, is to build a business case around a collection of use cases, or problems, that the proposed development would solve. The field of agriscience is no exception, and there is a long list of use cases where technology could be applied to assist farmers.

A use case, however, is inherently focused on the proposed development, as opposed to the betterment of the system into which it is implemented. The words themselves reveal this orientation: use case, or, flipped around, a case in which something could be used. The investment is thus focused on how something could be used, and a problem it could solve, as opposed to the betterment of the system in which it is implemented.

In the case of agricultural science, examining the application of machine learning to drone imagery through the lens of use cases, the value is inarguable. Through the lens of farmers in the United States, however, the average age of whom is over 60 and whose family has been farming their land for generations, a machine could never know the land better than they do. The investment and effort of researchers has solved a problem that no one was asking to be solved.

Whether or not machine learning can be applied to do something interesting has little to do with the future of an industry. Synthesis (which we will dive into more deeply later in this book) pivots the focus to the role or function that agriculture serves within its containing system (society): feeding the world.

To have a conversation with a farmer about feeding the world within the context of two of their larger systems, society and the earth itself and the changing climate conditions due to climate change, labor shortages now that the Internet has provided paths to digital jobs and there is a declining interest in farming, or the ever-growing global population, placing pressure for more food despite fewer farmers, one can lay the foundation for a discussion about the future of agriculture in which farmers would participate. Once the vision for the future of agriculture has been created, that vision can be disaggregated to understand the participation of individual farmers, agriscience companies, equipment manufacturers—the whole ecosystem that supports farming. In this context, investment in technologies would be focused on creating or improving parts of the broader system (agricultural) that the whole system has identified will be needed to improve the performance of the whole system at its function as a part of a broader system (feeding the world).

In this pivot, sales conversations no longer begin with the question of why a given development would be valuable, because its role in the future of that industry has already been defined, and it instead becomes a question of how well the development performs its function, at what price point, its ethical implications, and its ease of adoption.

The Second Use Case Problem: Use Case *Battleship*

Technologists reading this might have the question or thought about clients who ask for use cases, which is common in many industries as a lens through which new technologies can be easily examined.

When technologists approach business and industry leaders and managers, the application of technology is often framed within problems and use cases. There is considerable investment taking place at forward-thinking technology companies to pivot from product-based sales to outcome-based sales. This is an important evolution of the sales methodology to pivot salespersons from focusing on the applicability of their products to the necessary client impact, from which a line can (or cannot) be traced back to the products the salesperson is able to offer.

But this is still not enough if the organizational leader is focused on solving the next problem without designing to improve the whole system to which their organization contributes. If an organizational leader wants to improve efficiencies by a given percentage to counteract the ongoing decline of product sales, the resolution may actually be found in altering the product to increase sales or in improving customer experience to increase retention. It is the responsibility of organizational leaders to realize when they are caught in the problem-solving loop and pause to reassess strategy. In the absence of an organizational leadership capability to pause and reassess, the responsibility falls to their team and advisors to have the insight to identify this phenomenon and the bravery or vulnerability to raise it to their leaders.

When clients request use cases examples, sometimes the intent is to illuminate the capability of a technology, which can lead to a discussion about its ability to solve a different use case. Other times, they are playing "Use Case *Battleship*." *Battleship* is a two-player board game in which the players can only see their own set of ships and submarines on an algebraic grid. They take turns calling "shots" into the other player's side of the board by naming algebraic squares. The other player then notifies them whether the shot is a hit or a miss.

Some clients wait for technology providers to name the right square on their invisible grid and, in its worst form, accumulate collections of point solutions solving individual use cases from different vendors, creating a bloated and disconnected overarching system that performs the same or worse than it would without those solutions.

This has become one of the largest challenges facing the modern organization.

If the concept of a human did not exist, and those tasked with creating a human first solved the problem of movement, then the problem of reproduction, and then of generating energy, the resulting system would be unrecognizable. Taken a step further, if the human body were a technological entity, and the development of each function of the human body were assigned to different technology providers on different technology stacks, there would be a high likelihood that many of the parts of the human body would not interact with one another.

Doing the Wrong Thing Right

Packing into a car with family or friends for a leisurely road trip across a country or continent is an exciting prospect. Innately, road trips include a balance of planning and spontaneity. Even the most thought-through plan can be thwarted by weather conditions, road closures, or spotting an unanticipated landmark and stopping along the way.

Some road trips swing in the opposite direction and intentionally begin without a plan, embracing spontaneity and approaching each leg of the trip as an adventure.

An organizational initiative shares many similarities with a road trip. Someone has to drive, the vehicle can only go so far without further investment, everyone must agree to go to the same place, and the best-laid plan will inevitably meet surprises, often requiring a reevaluation of the plan.

One of the challenges faced by organizations today occurs when organizational leaders state where they want to go at the onset of a new trip, but before programming the GPS with the destination to generate a route, they create a list of problems that need to be solved: fill up the car with gas (or charge it), use the restroom, get snacks, get coffee, stop to stretch legs, stop for lunch—many hours can pass by, routing at each point toward the next problem to be solved, but without connection to the long-term destination or strategy, valuable time and energy has been wasted. If challenged on this approach, the leader might reply that each of those stops is a necessary part of a road trip, and they would be right. Every road trip includes stopping for food, gas, and snacks, but if those take place outside the context of the broader route, a trip that should take two days could take weeks, or worse—and, more often than not when it comes to technology initiatives, never arrive at the destination.

There are many reasons this could be the case, such as the innate desire to check items off a checklist or the organizational need to demonstrate progress each quarter.

But demonstrating progress toward the wrong goal or outside the context of a long-term strategy is counterproductive, or, as the late Dr. Russell Ackoff, a former Wharton professor and organizational theorist, said, "The righter we do the wrong thing, the wronger we become. When we make a mistake doing the wrong thing and correct it, we become wronger. When we make a mistake doing the right thing and correct it, we become righter. Therefore, it is better to do the right thing wrong than the wrong thing right."[2]

Organizations have a natural aptitude for correcting mistakes without examining whether that process is doing the right or wrong thing for the organization in the long term.

If a process is found to have an inefficiency, and an analysis demonstrates that the process can be streamlined to improve efficiency by 2% by the end of the quarter with a reasonable investment of capital and resources, it becomes an obvious choice for a leader. Teams or consultants will be assigned to search for similar problems to be solved. If the work is performed well, the leader can submit a report that includes the percentage of increased efficiency produced by their team's work, the cost reduction, or the increased profit. This becomes a positive performance review, justifying bonuses and increased budgetary allocation to that leader's organization.

Many leaders have risen through organizations by creating a demonstrable record of solving problems.

This becomes a vicious cycle and can lead to narrowing the aperture for organizational investment of time and resources to solving problems with a preference for the problems that will demonstrate the best numbers within a quarter or fiscal year as opposed to whether or not they are contributing to the performance of the overarching organization or should be scrapped or redesigned altogether, which would likely not yield demonstrable efficiency gains within a given quarter or fiscal year.

The pursuit of short-term, demonstrable results is taught in school and reinforced by current economic incentives within organizations because most leaders and managers must answer for the demonstrable, measurable results achieved by their team or organization in quarterly reviews and at the end of each fiscal year.

This systemic context is one of the primary reasons technology initiatives fail and organizations and society face unrealized economic potential.

Notes

1. Open Learn, "Wrong Thing Righter?," Section 1.9 in Organisations, Environmental Management and Innovation course, The Open University, https://www.open.edu/openlearn/nature-environment/organisations-environmental-management-and-innovation/content-section-1.9.
2. Open Learn, "Wrong Thing Righter?," Section 1.9 in Organisations, Environmental Management and Innovation course, The Open University, https://www.open.edu/openlearn/nature-environment/organisations-environmental-management-and-innovation/content-section-1.9.

CHAPTER 7

Developing the Skill of Envisioning

Envisioning the future is not a talent or gift, but a skill that can be developed. Those who are particularly skilled at envisioning the future are often attributed with the gift of vision and genius, like modern-day oracles.

As someone who has spent decades developing the skill of envisioning the future, both individually and in collaboration with others, and who so deeply enjoys the process that colleagues and friends have coined the state of mind that I venture into ("Brianstorming"), I can say firsthand that the process is deeply personal, vulnerable, and can be developed like any other skill.

Envisioning is deeply personal in the sense that it necessitates the personal experiences and synaptic connections of an individual in order for the result to have relevance in the context of the individual, organization, industry, and/or market for which the envisioning is developed. You cannot pay someone else, regardless of their degree of skill in the process of envisioning, to adequately envision your future or the future of your organization. Organizational leaders must develop the process of envisioning the future, both individually and collaboratively, if their organization is going to reach, retain, or expand a market leadership position and create lasting value. From a social systemic viewpoint, this process of envisioning the future, as opposed to having it envisioned for them by external advisors, also serves as a foundation of mutual buy-in that can sustain momentum when challenges arise.

Envisioning is a vulnerable act of creation—of imagination, a distinctively human skill, and a skill that can be observed under development in any child. For adults, envisioning becomes vulnerable in that it begins with an admission that the future is unknowable and therefore cannot be controlled, and, like any act of creation, exposes an individual's thinking process or line of reasoning to others. This is one of the reasons it is important that organizations transition to operating as social systems instead of mechanistic systems, in which empathy, reason, vulnerability, and candor are seen as skills as valuable as data science, project management, or engineering.

In terms of skill development, envisioning the future is a recursive activity, with lengthy feedback loops, and it can be developed in the same way as any other skill. No rational person, in considering a software engineer who has written a particularly elegant function in JavaScript, would assert that some people were just born to write code and that the oracles blessed them with innate programming talents. That developer had to learn the syntax of writing code and the theory, and then practice over weeks, months, and years to develop the skill to the point that it culminates in elegant code. This is not to say that individuals do not have natural aptitudes that lend themselves to particular skills, but that those skills are not deterministic at birth but can be developed even after childhood.

The skill of envisioning the future is developed in the same manner as the skills of writing software or project management: a combination of theory and practice. There are many thought leaders who have written about both the theory and the practice of creating a vision for the future (some of whose books can be found in the "What Should You Read Next?" section at the end of this book), and advisory firms can be hired to serve as guides and facilitators for technology, business, and industry leaders steeped in the social systemic context of an organization in order to envision a future for the team, organization, market, and industry.

Once a future vision, or a set of several future scenarios, has been developed, it can then be traced backward to the starting point of the present to determine what needs to be in place to achieve that future vision, then create a plan for growing from the starting point to the other without losing the pieces that made the culture great in the first place. As Mark Hammond, the founder of Bons.ai, an autonomous artificial intelligence platform acquired by Microsoft in 2018, describes it, "It is not a replacement operation, it's a growth operation."

Functional Reimagining

Every person, team, organization, and ecosystem serves a function within one or more broader systems. Functional reimagining is a creative process that begins with an examination of what part the subject of the creative process, such as an organization, serves within its broader containing systems. These systems could be the overarching organization, the market, the industry, the education system, and society (to name a few).

A team that delivers a daily report to leadership on a given aspect of the organization, for example, is not a reporting function. Reporting is the method by which the team delivers on its core function of informing the daily decisions of leadership with information about the organization. Depending on the context of the organization, there are many ways in which this team could be functionally reimagined.

Functional reimagining in this context would begin with a deeper understanding of what decisions are being made by leadership on a daily basis and what information is needed to inform those decisions. From a social systemic viewpoint, for example, each leader has a style in which they best consume and interact with information. Some leaders may want a daily bulleted list of key metrics. Another leader might prefer a 15-minute morning readout of the state of the business with summarized insights and an ongoing discussion with an internal analyst who serves as an advisor. Another leader with a background in data analytics might want access to a self-serve business intelligence dashboard. Beginning with this context in mind informs the process of envisioning possible future scenarios, and what combination of reports, dashboards, and interaction between the team and the leaders it supports would best fulfill its core function within the broader system.

Zoomed out to the context of an entire organization, a core function might be to clothe people for formal events. This function plays a part within every sector, including, as examples, the fashion, entertainment, public, and private sectors. Reimagining the performance of this function would begin with an understanding of the current social systemic context of clothing people for formal events, which, after the COVID-19 pandemic, may consist of fewer events than before the pandemic. Additionally, some might be meeting team members, colleagues, or industry peers for the first time post-pandemic, and therefore be willing to spend more for higher-quality items. Furthermore, due to the social impact of the pandemic in regard to increased comfort with shopping online and waiting for shipping, paired with store closures and low inventory, lowering the likelihood or confidence in venturing to an in-person store, the ability to purchase fashion items that can be shipped to one's home might be worth a cost premium to enough consumers to justify a reimagining of the methods by which the organization fulfills its core function in society. Each of these is a hypothesis that would need to be proved or disproved in order to meaningfully contribute to overarching theories of how the organization can best fulfill its core function, the process of which will be covered in Chapter 15.

Multiverse Reimagining

The multiverse is a theoretical group of multiple parallel universes, often depicted within science fiction with subtle differences that accrue to uncanny experiences for those who can travel between them.

Imagine waking up in a parallel universe in which your house is the same, all of the same people exist with the same history and relationships, with the one difference being that the team and/or organization you work in or lead does not exist. No one has ever heard of your team or organization, except for a benefactor who has given you the charter to build the team or organization from scratch. You look up your colleagues online and see that they all have different jobs at other organizations, with no mention of your team or organization in their work history.

What would you build? This creative process also begins with considering the function the team and organization performs within its containing systems, and requires a social systemic lens to consider the roles and motivations of the humans that comprise the team and social systems of the organization and the broader containing systems.

Once a future vision of the organization has been developed, the process of discovering and rediscovering the context of the system, clearing the digital fog, designing for inevitability, and creating a more human future can begin.

PART FOUR

Discover and Rediscover

We shall not cease from exploration

And the end of all our exploring

Will be to arrive where we started

And know the place for the first time.

—T. S. ELIOT, IN *FOUR QUARTETS*

CHAPTER 8

Systemic Design and the Lost Art of Synthesis

As individuals and organizations, there are three ways to move into the future. The distinction between them lies in their ability to effect outcomes, without an assignment of moral or ethical obligation. The first is passive, watching as the future unfolds day by day. The second is active, responding to change and charting a course from one problem to the next. The third is also active, imagining a future in which the individual or organization would like to exist, and designing the means by which that future may be actualized.

Although some organizations and leaders are moving passively into the future, the default setting is reacting to change. This results in backing into the future rather than advancing into it, and justifying action only in response to a problem. There is evidence of this scattered through organizational presentations, startup pitch decks, and marketing collateral. Investments are justified in response to changing market conditions, competitive headwinds, or increased prices.

The COVID-19 pandemic is a perfect example of this dynamic in action. Organizations that had either been unwilling or unable to empower employees to work remotely mobilized almost overnight. Organizations whose core competencies were adjacent to a need arising from the pandemic retooled their warehouses and approved investment plans in a fraction of the time and with less information than ever before. Organizations and individuals who believe in taking action are naturally good at responding to change and reacting to a problem.

Investments in emerging technologies follow the same pattern. Most discussions with organizational leaders about emerging technologies start or end with a review or question of what other companies have invested in and seen results from the technology.

Consider your own organization. What was your most recent investment in an emerging technology? What was the justification? Were competitors considered? Trends? In other words, was the investment a response to change or was it by design?

In 2004, when Steve Jobs decided to invest in developing the iPhone, it was not in response to competitors. Although the original concept of a smartphone had been conceived 15 years prior, Jobs's decision was focused on designing a future in which Apple strengthened its leadership position in the market, building on its core competencies and existing products.

Ironically, organizations responded to Apple's success by hiring designers at senior levels in hopes of recreating that success within their market sector. Harold Nelson, a founder of the discipline of systemic design, points out that "adding designers to the senior leadership was not enough to recreate Apple's success. Existing leaders, with domain expertise specific to their sectors, needed to gain the systemic design skill set as Steve Jobs did."

Many organizations have begun holding design thinking workshops and hiring management consultants for leadership retreats or off-sites. Too often, however, although these are viewed positively and generate excitement, the design thinking ends when leaders and managers return to their offices or homes, and despite a high degree of excitement and great ideas, the ideas are not translated to meaningful investments in changing the course of the organization.

The challenge that has faced organizations throughout the era of Digital Transformation and must be overcome in order to harness the opportunity presented by the era of Autonomous Transformation is that these design thinking workshops are often designed to define the ends, but not the means.

If a leadership team decides to invest in a set of visionary goals, with their sights on achieving Profitable Good, but do not change the means by which the organization endeavors toward that outcome, even though they may attain a return on their investments, it will be a small fraction of what it could have been.

Microsoft's journey from 2014 through 2022 is an example of this in action. When Satya Nadella stepped into the chief executive office, although the goals of the business did shift, that alone would not have led to Microsoft's successful reemergence as a market leader. It was the change of the means by which Microsoft did business that made its transformation possible. When Joe Whittinghill was brought into Satya Nadella's office to accept the request that he transition from his role managing Mergers and Acquisitions to leading the company's culture transformation, given his years of experience studying companies and industries, Satya told him, "We need to change our technology strategy, our business strategy, and our people strategy."

Organizational leaders at this juncture must be cautious of the appeal to authority fallacy. Academic leaders, researchers, consultants, and leaders from other organizations cannot design the future state of the organization for you. They may be able to teach you or guide you through the process of designing your transformation, reformation, and new acts of creation, but none of them know your business, your culture, your customers, or your domain like you and your fellow organizational leaders do. Steve Jobs co-founded Apple and deeply understood its business, technology, and industry. Satya Nadella worked at Microsoft for 22 years before he became chief executive officer. This is not to say that an external leader cannot join an organization and lead it into a new era, but that a necessary ingredient in its transformation, reformation, and new acts of creation is deep expertise of its business, technology, industry, and culture. In other words, the leader needs to understand the overarching system of the business, for which an externally sourced leader will need to lean heavily on their leadership team.

Real design is hard, and requires investment beyond money, in a different way of thinking and working. People have sunk costs in the way they have been taught to think and their patterns of thinking have been shaped by the way they have been rewarded.

Leaders often pose the question: What will the organization look like in 10 years? This fosters a discussion and potentially even investment in researching trends to attempt to answer this question. But the bigger question is: What do you want it to be?

In 1876, Thomas Edison set a goal to produce one major invention every six months and one minor invention every 10 days. This was not a reaction to trends or a competitive analysis. Edison was creating components that would come to transform the future. Embracing uncertainty, he and his team focused on directional milestones instead of outcomes. Whether or not an invention is produced within a given time period is a directional measurement of progress, and not a measurement of outcomes. A measurement of outcomes, such as the ability for those inventions to result in profit, for example, would have stifled the inventive process. Directional milestones allowed Edison and his vertically integrated research and development lab to continue inventing and to subsequently double down on the inventions that demonstrated a likelihood of yielding profits.

For anyone who has been a part of or had visibility into artificial intelligence or emerging technology initiatives, there is a pattern of a lack of design for the broader system and/or the focus on achieving specific return on investment outcomes within a short timeline.

Humans do not tend to do this in other arenas. In romantic relationships, human beings follow directional milestones to see if the relationship will last long term. If, at the onset of a relationship, one partner were to outline the timeline in which they needed to realize a return on the relationship in order to proceed, a second date would be unlikely.

Humankind's exploration into outer space has been based on directional milestones. If return on investment had been a requirement in the Space Race, the space program would have been shut down long before astronauts took their first steps on the moon. Yet many of the technological and organizational advancements benefiting society and businesses today were invented to support the Apollo missions.

Not every business has the luxury of being able to explore. Some organizations, culturally, financially, or otherwise, can only invest in systems and technologies that have reached a point of such ubiquity that investments carry little risk and a dependable return on investment.

The uncomfortable truth is paradoxical. Many of these technologies are still in the exploratory phase of real-world application, and yet there is enough signal in the market that those who do not invest in these technologies are choosing to disregard a considerable degree of untapped economic potential and the risk of their business facing an unavoidable existential threat before the risk of investment has lowered to their preferred tolerance level.

The Interconnectedness of Parts within a System

Two of the most accurate predictors of whether an artificial intelligence or other emerging technological initiative will fail are when they are funded and managed on the basis of return on investment and timelines as opposed to directional milestones, and when they are designed within and for individual parts of a system and not for the system as a whole.

Throughout the process of designing and leading creative, reformational, and transformational initiatives across a business or within a team, it is critical for organizational leaders and managers to begin building the skill of systemic design, which starts with understanding three key principles of systems:

1. Each part of a system can affect the defining behavior or properties of the whole and is necessary for it.
2. None of the essential parts can have an independent effect on the defining function(s) of the whole.
3. No subgroup of the essential parts can have an independent effect on the defining function(s) of the whole.

A system is a whole that cannot be divided into independent parts. Since the parts interact, the properties of the system are a product of the interaction of the parts, not the parts taken separately. When you improve the performance of each part of the system taken separately, you do not improve the performance of the system taken as a whole.

This can be proven within the systems sciences, and also through a thought experiment. Imagine that an organization, in search of re-engineering the best possible computer, purchases the top computer from every computer manufacturer in existence. They have those computers shipped to a large warehouse and hire top experts to study them. They determine which computer has the best monitor, which has the best processing unit, which has the best sound system, which has the best power cable, and so on. They examine the computers piece by piece until they have a list of all the best individual parts. Next, they proceed to take each of those parts out of their individual computers and put them all together into a new computer. Do they have the newest supercomputer? Does it even turn on? Absolutely not, because the performance of the system is based on the interaction between parts and not the individual parts by themselves.

In another context, if an Olympic swimmer trained each individual muscle involved in swimming with targeted weight-lifting and breathing exercises, but never trained the interaction between the parts by practicing swimming, how well would they perform?

Creative, reformational, and transformational initiatives must necessarily be focused on re-engineering the interactions between the parts of the organization, between teams, organizations, and technological systems, with customers, and with partners. Although it appears intuitive to optimize individual parts of the system, such as an individual, a team, or a technological system, without treatment of the interaction between those parts, the system will not improve. Moreover, the exercise weighs the organization down and increases the risk of burnout.

Ragu Athinarayanan, professor and director of Purdue University's Smart Manufacturing Innovation Center, advises organizations all over the world on initiatives related to manufacturing, technology, and management. His feedback on why investments in Digital Transformation have struggled to achieve the anticipated returns was that "many of the false starts I see on transformation, they say 'I want to solve one problem at a time,' rather than building a transformation strategy at the board level."

This articulates the pervasive misunderstanding that a system can be improved by improving and optimizing its individual components. This was considered true in a Taylorism context, but it was ultimately proven to be false because the system of the organization could not survive the impact of worker burnout. This is also false in the context of software engineering, where it almost seems to be true. Reducing the latency of an individual Application Programming Interface (API) call, on the surface, would improve the performance of the system. A lack of consideration of that API call's interaction with other parts of the system, however, could result in a bug because a function triggered by the return of that data began earlier than intended. A software engineer could and should argue that this should not be the case and that the function should be updated to accommodate the reduced latency. This is systems thinking, as the software engineer is designing for the interaction between these individual parts to improve the whole. Software applications are a fertile environment for systems thinking, as the feedback loop is immediate. Tuning an individual component at the expense of the system results in an error or a bug the next time the code is compiled.

Unlike the disciplines of software engineering or the built environment, where feedback is immediate, an adjustment to an individual part of an organization that negatively impacts the performance of the broader organization is likely to go unnoticed in the short term and remain undetected in organizational performance assessments. This increases the responsibility of leaders and managers to design and lead initiatives as well as their teams and organizations within the context of the broader system, focused on managing interaction and not action.

In a conversation with a leader in research intelligence at one of the largest agriscience institutes, he highlighted the challenge of technology adoption in the agricultural sector, which follows the pattern of focusing on parts of the system and not the interaction of various parts within the system as a whole.

Organizations large and small have invested in remote sensing, satellite imagery, and developing drones to capture real-time data on the ground in a particular growing area. Digital tools have been developed for farmers to recommend the right timing for applying nitrogen or water, and assisting in identifying crops that are diseased or damaged by insects. These are optimizations of a part of the system. The other part of the system is farmers, who have been farming their whole life, are experts in their craft, and are not interested in technology or algorithms telling them how to manage their farms. Culturally, more than many other occupations, their work is intertwined with their family history and sense of identity. Had these same investments started with the interaction between parts of the system, in other words, taken farmers and their cultural and ideological context into account in the design of the system, more value may have been realized with less investment.

Dimensions of Systems

A system is inextricable from the matrix in which it develops. A matrix is defined as "the cultural, social, or political environment in which something develops."[1] This makes it critical for leaders and managers to foster an agility to understand the ongoing multidimensionality of their organizations or teams. Each organization is founded within a specific political, social, and cultural context. The founders and their initial team created a system in which the organization continued to develop. As the matrix around the organization evolves, the organization will naturally evolve as well. When leaders are unattuned to this dynamic, they run the risk of the organization evolving in unproductive or even harmful ways. The antithesis of this is leaders and managers who purposely adjust the matrix of their organization to create the best possible environment for the culture and value creation they are pursuing.

If the demographic or social identity of a team or organization is representative of one or two primary people groups when it is small, for example, it is important to add new voices as it grows to create the strongest conditions for innovation. I have seen this in my own work, in the proposal phase of a technology project within the built environment (specifically the construction of buildings). The project team consisted of highly skilled technologists and consultants, and I was asked to contribute to the analytics portion, which my practice would be responsible for executing if our firm won the project. When I reviewed the proposal, I could not help but read the whole proposal, justifying to myself that it would inform the analytics portion of the proposal. My father was a general contractor, and I spent many childhood weekends and school breaks traveling to building sites with him, so I was curious. It became clear within the first paragraphs that none of the team members who had designed this solution had ever worn a toolbelt, as several components of the proposal relied on assumptions of the environment of a construction site that were false. If an expert in the built environment had been involved in the design phase of the proposal, not only would the solution have been tenable, but the ideas put forth could have truly pushed the envelope of what is possible in the built environment through the application of technology.

In this example, diversity of expertise and experience would have made a material difference in the outcome of tens of thousands of dollars of firm investment in pursuing the creation of a proposal. This is even more critical when building a new product or evolving a product or solution to accommodate the ever-changing social, cultural, and political environment.

There is no innovation process or compliance checklist that can measure up to diversity of expertise, diversity of knowledge, diversity of lived experience, and diversity of applied experience. These become force multipliers when added to a team or organization.

The organizations that are thriving in today's market are those that, by accident, urgency, or (less frequently) by design, hired "nontraditional" candidates, who later proved, in combination with team members with more traditional experience, to create positive friction, which is the most fertile environment for innovation and growth.

The organization and its products, processes, and culture will evolve continuously, either as a reaction to the ongoing shifts in the social, cultural, and political environment in which it exists, or by design. Some changes cannot be anticipated, such as the sudden lockdowns that began in response to the COVID-19 pandemic. Organizations were not given the opportunity to design for this situation, and had to react in real time.

Within that same context, however, lay a cultural shift that organizations continue to struggle to address: return to work in person, hybrid work, remote work, the Great Resignation, and the Great Reshuffle. In the face of a significant degree of signal from employees and the broader market, an overwhelming number of organizations have chosen to wait and react to further developments.

Many organizations that reacted quickly to employee questions regarding the organization's post-pandemic work flexibility policies by communicating their plan to require in-person participation for knowledge workers lost talent to organizations that were vocal about their workplace flexibility policies and posted fully remote roles.

Even though the signal came early that workers did not want to return to the office, many leaders either decreed plans to return to the office or chose to wait to get more information. Others designed policies they felt met their business objective while also attracting and retaining top talent, because the matrix in which the organization existed—the market—had evolved throughout the pandemic, and organizations needed to adapt.

From a "leaders as designers" perspective, this contemporary discourse is an important example. There are currently three main approaches circulating: fully remote, fully in-person, and hybrid—typically one to three days in the office and the rest remote.

Given the new global context in which many talented people from all over the world moved home to be with their families during the pandemic, finally moved to that remote town they had always dreamed of moving to, remodeled their home offices, or consolidated cars, organizations that require even one day in the office narrow the available workforce, contrasted with the total number of working-age individuals worldwide. For some organizations, this is not different than their pre-pandemic situation, in which, due to in-person policies, they could only hire local or willing-to-move talent. Other organizations approached the pandemic as an opportunity to tap into the global workforce like never before.

Leaders who understand the systems of their organization, market, and value chains and then design the future from within that context will be able to lead their organizations through hardships and disruptions, sustaining the organization's ability to create value.

The Lost Art of Synthesis

Analysis and *synthesis* are terms that are used widely, and in many contexts and disciplines. The prevalence of analysis, combined with the increased ability to apply analytical methods at scale through computing, has left synthesis in the background, lost to many organizational leaders, despite its relevance.

In the context of systems thinking, analysis is the process by which a system is taken apart to acquire knowledge of how it works. Synthesis is the inverse, which begins its examination of a system with the question of what function it serves as a part of a larger, containing system to gain an understanding of why the system exists.

In the context of organizational leadership and management, synthesis is as important as analysis for creating, reforming, and transforming organizations, which, at their root, are social systems that perform specific functions within broader systems such as the market, the nations in which they operate, and society.

The three steps of the process of analysis (as visualized in Figure 8.1) within the field of systems thinking, as defined by the late Dr. Russell Ackoff, a former Wharton professor and organizational theorist (previously mentioned in Chapter 6), are as follows:

1. Take [a subject] apart and examine its parts.
2. Try to understand each part taken separately.
3. Aggregate an understanding of the parts into an understanding of the whole.

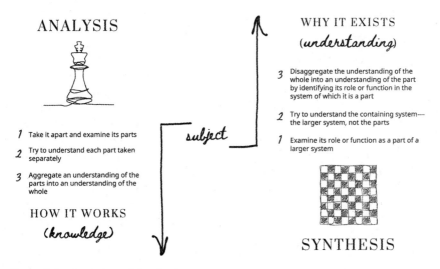

Figure 8.1   Analysis and Synthesis

The application of analysis to a modern bank would begin with taking it apart and examining its parts. It may be made up of a website, an application, and branches, through which it offers financial products such as lines of credit, mortgages, loans, credit cards, and checking and savings accounts. Further analysis would seek to understand each of these parts individually, such as the function of a checking account, the function of a credit card, and so on. Once a satisfactory understanding of each part taken separately has been reached, the next step is to aggregate an understanding of each part into an understanding of the bank as a whole. The analysis would have revealed knowledge such as the number of customers, the total amount of extended credit, the risk profiles of borrowers, and the average traffic to the bank's website and mobile application contrasted with in-person visits to the physical locations.

When it is time for a board meeting, none of these details can answer the question as to the performance of the bank in its core function. They can provide an understanding of how individual parts of the bank are performing within their subfunctions, and this might be enough for some boards, but the process of synthesis, in combination with analysis, is the only basis for answering the question of how an organization is performing in its core function.

The three steps of the process of synthesis within the field of systems thinking are:

1. Examine [a subject's] role or function as part of a larger system.
2. Try to understand the containing system—the larger system, not the parts.
3. Disaggregate the understanding of the whole into an understanding of the part by identifying its role or function in the system of which it is a part.[2]

Returning to the analogy of a bank, the first step of synthesis is examining its role or function as a part of a larger system. Depending on where they are located, banks serve a role or function in a capitalist, socialist, or other economic system, but can also be examined as a part of the larger system of society.

If one wanted to consider the idea of decentralized banking, the process of analysis can only reveal knowledge about the difference between a decentralized bank and centralized banks and the underlying technology of blockchain and its utility in supporting a decentralized bank.

Synthesis is the means of moving beyond knowledge to develop an understanding of whether a decentralized bank would better serve the function of a bank within the context of an economic system or society, as it examines the function a bank serves within those containing systems, which can then be examined for their functions, such as supporting the welfare of the people within them, and an understanding of the function of society and the function of economic systems can then be disaggregated into an understanding of the role or function a bank plays within those broader systems. This can then be used to inform discussions about how changes to the banking system would impact its ability to serve its core function within its broader containing systems.

In the pursuit of applying advanced technologies within organizations to improve the performance of an organization, the process of analysis only yields knowledge of how the technology works, how much it costs, and how it might be applied within that organization. Investments made purely on the basis of analysis, even when they yield the targeted results, run the risk (which is observed too often in practice) of only improving the performance of the individual suborganization, and not the organization as a whole.

Synthesis provides a counterbalance to analysis, providing an understanding of why a given suborganization exists within the broader containing organization, which can then be leveraged to inform investments to improve the suborganization's ability to perform its core function and interact with other suborganizations to improve the performance of the organization as a whole.

Notes

1. "Matrix," Oxford Learner's Dictionaries,
   https://www.oxfordlearnersdictionaries.com/definition/english/matrix?q=matrix.
2. Russell Ackoff and Kellie Wardman, "From Mechanistic to Social Systemic Thinking," Systems Thinker, https://thesystemsthinker.com/from-mechanistic-to-social-systemic-thinking/.

CHAPTER **9**

The Organization as a Chessboard: Seeing the Pieces

W hen I was 12 years old, I won $565 at a casino in Nevada, where the United States National Open Chess Tournament was held. I had tied for first place in my rating category after a grueling eight-hour match against a man several times my age and experience. I secured the victory when he doubled down and narrowed his focus of the board and pieces to his line of attack. Chess players are constantly reminded, whether through direct teaching or the experience of loss, to consider the entire board and resist the temptation to get tunnel vision on winning a piece or gaining positional advantage.

The first time I experienced this in a business context was when I was building an organization that taught chess to students at private and public schools. Our model passed the cost of the program on to families, which meant that any school that did not already have an after-school chess program was likely to be open to seeing if we could generate enough interest to start a program (this also inflated my perception of my sales abilities at the time). Our program was flourishing at private schools and economically advantaged public schools.

Where we struggled was in getting enough paying students at schools in economically disadvantaged districts, and one of our business mentors recommended that we research districts and target those with higher degrees of economic advantage. It did not sit right with me or my co-founder that the program we had built to increase children's critical thinking and creative skills would only be available to students who already had access to other valuable educational resources and after-school programs. The system was set against the economically disadvantaged students, and our not being able to offer our programs to them was one example. So we decided that we would try a new approach to reach those students. We modeled it out and determined that for every five paying schools, we would be able to offer our program for free to one school.

We contacted schools in economically disadvantaged districts and offered our program for free. Several schools took us up on our offer, and one principal asked us if we knew about Title I, a federal program that provides funding to schools that serve an economically disadvantaged area with the goal of supplementing instruction to increase academic growth. In the analogy of seeing the whole chessboard, this was a piece we were unaware was on the board. We reengineered our program to operate at narrow enough margins that we could maintain a small but dependable profit by scaling our business through Title I funding, landing considerably more impact than we would have been able to with our initial plan. This was an accidental yet fortuitous opportunity for Profitable Good. Within a couple years, our business had swung in the direction of teaching at more economically disadvantaged schools than private schools and people joined our organization just to have the opportunity to work with these students.

Many years and several career moves later, I was in a design thinking session with a client who was considering building a platform that would rely on data from building management systems (i.e., the systems that control and monitor the building's mechanical and electrical equipment such as ventilation, lighting, power, fire, and security systems). The proposed plan of action for validating whether this platform idea was worth further exploration was to check if the building management system organizations allowed their data to be accessed via an application programming interface (API).

I thought for a moment and asked if we should also consider reaching out to the building management systems organizations directly to see if they would be interested in forming a partnership in which we paid for access to their data, which we could build into our model, and if they would invest in building custom API integrations with our client's platform. With a little bit of research, we discovered that there were only a handful of building management systems organizations serving the majority of the market, so it would require only a few discussions to validate the idea.

The client remarked that they never would have thought of reaching out to the building management systems organizations. In terms of systems, they would have accepted the state of the system, whether that meant they would have API access or not, and subsequently ended exploration of their idea if it did not fit into the existing system.

This stuck with me, and I made a point of noticing whenever a colleague, client, or partner was narrowed in on a subset of the broader system; to my surprise, it was almost everywhere I looked.

Early on in this book, I shared the example of the large public utility company focused on stopping deregulation of the utilities sector, and how I raised the idea of creating a self-generation offering that could be tested in countries that are not regulated and states that have gone through the process of deregulation. This could lead to a global leadership position in the future of the energy sector. When I brought this idea up, the C-level executives in the room for that discussion looked at one another with surprise before one of them spoke up and shared that this idea had not been considered or discussed within their leadership team.

How to Determine Whether You Are Focused on a Subset of the Whole System

Leaders and managers are presented with challenges on a daily, if not multiple times per day, basis. These challenges can be related to talent, clients or customers, competitors, partners, suppliers, public relations, organizational changes, leadership transitions—it is a long list.

Leaders who see the whole system understand their organization's unique position in the market, and they understand what motivates their team members, what kind of surprising and remarkable partnerships they should set in motion, which emerging technologies to invest in, and which to monitor as they make further developments.

The determining factor as to whether you see the whole system comes down to what pieces you see on the board when facing a problem, whether you examine the pieces when you are not facing a problem, your ability to identify the leverage points, and the degree to which you consider the pieces movable.

Returning to the previous example, the leaders exploring building a platform that would rely on building management system data did not see the "partner directly with the building management system organization" piece, and they considered the pieces outside their organization immovable.

For the utilities organization and the question of deregulation, they did not see the "build a strategy to treat deregulation as an opportunity" piece on the board; they were not examining the pieces at their disposal outside the context of a problem. On the contrary, they were only planning to examine those pieces and set their strategy if and when the problem became urgent, and they had not examined whether the pieces within their own system were movable.

An example of seeing a whole system that had yet to exist is the story of Henry Ford. Henry Ford is famous for having said "If I had asked people what they wanted, they would have said faster horses." Ford existed within a system in which the first car had been created by Carl Benz in Germany 10 years before Ford made his first car. After successfully creating a working car, Ford founded two car companies that failed. The economic system had rejected the ideas Ford was determined to manifest in the market. The system that existed before cars was such that only the elite and bourgeoisie could afford carriages. Even in the act of innovating vehicles, the predominant trend was to create large, heavy cars that were expensive to purchase and maintain. Ford saw a piece on the board that no one else saw or was willing to believe existed. He believed that inexpensive cars would sell to a mass market and create the precursor to the modern road trip or afternoon drive. This generated a network effect because once you start making inexpensive cars, people want to buy more inexpensive cars, and once people want to buy more inexpensive cars, there are going to be gas stations, and once there are gas stations and Disneyland, we need more inexpensive cars, and then the next thing you know, you have paved the planet.

There are two other stories about Henry Ford in which he did not see or understand the full system. The first is in a lesser-known story about a town called Fordlandia, which Ford founded in Brazil in an attempt to source rubber for tires directly to remove reliance on suppliers. He believed he could do good in Brazil and, misguided by his lack of insight into the full system, he required workers and their families to adopt American ways of living, dressing, grooming, working, and even dancing. Had he seen and understood the broader system of Brazil, understood his workers' motivations and the conditions in which they would thrive, and celebrated and honored their culture, the project might have had turned out differently. Instead, it ended in riots and the abandonment of the project.

The second story about Henry Ford in which he did not see or understand the full system can be found in his descent into anti-Semitism, the ideas of which he published in a series of articles in the Dearborn *Independent* from 1920 to 1922. While a deeper understanding of the full system may not have altered his troublesome beliefs, a lack of understanding of the system is evident in his writings of the time.[1]

What is your organization's core competency? This question can be asked of any leader or manager, and their answer will elucidate their understanding of their team and organization within the broader system or marketplace.

Tim Linsenmeyer is the chief technology officer at Clover Imaging Group, an organization that manufactures most of the printer ink cartridges sold in the United States. When I asked Tim what Clover Imaging Group's core competency was, his answer was unexpected: picking and shipping—in other words, warehouse operations and logistics. With the rise of digital systems, be it electronic contracts, emails replacing faxes, or digital photo albums mounted in homes around the world, leaders in the printing business need to start considering their long-term strategies. Tim Linsenmeyer and Clover are already in the process of reinventing themselves. They have packaged their remanufacturing capabilities together with their core competencies of picking and shipping to enable other businesses to outsource their man-ufacturing to Clover to focus on *their* core competencies. Because Clover's core competency is picking and shipping, they focus investments in building technological capabilities to make these competencies even stronger, and they partner with technology companies and closely monitor their build-versus-buy strategy.

Tim's vision also includes Profitable Good. He and his team invested in fusing their core competency together with artificial intelligence to create a system for empowering individuals with disabilities to pick in a warehousing context. He partnered with Gigi's Playhouse, a nonprofit organization that provides free educational, therapeutic, and career development programs for individuals with Down syndrome, their families, and the community, to test the system and hire individuals with Down syndrome. When faced with the challenge of how to arrange transportation for these new team members to and from the warehouse, he and his team examined the broader system and identified an organization with a core competency in mobility: a ride-sharing company. Clover formed a deal with a ride-sharing company that scheduled drivers to transport Clover's new team members for $1.50 each way. This chesspiece was not even on the board, but Tim's passion and the vision of the initiative created a piece where there was none. Two weeks later, these new team members received their first paychecks and Tim's team began working on open-sourcing the technology for others to be able to hire individuals with disabilities. You can access the code repository online.[2]

The first step in uncovering a system is identifying the pieces on the board and how they move. Connected circles, an exercise stemming from the disciplines of systems thinking and systemic design, provides a framework for beginning this process. Figure 9.1 shares an example of the first step of draw-ing the circle and writing down two or three elements (or pieces).

The connected circle of the contemporary state of artificial intelligence begins with the unrealized economic opportunity of artificial intelligence. The technology has passed the inflection point to the degree that organiza-tional leaders are exploring or planning to explore applications of artificial intelligence within their organizations. The second piece on the board, which organizations discovered almost immediately upon researching the field of artificial intelligence, is the limited number of data scientists. This scarcity follows the classic economic model of supply and demand, resulting in the high cost of artificial intelligence initiatives.

Figure 9.2 demonstrates the second step of adding additional elements of the system to the circle. The goal in this step is not to be comprehensive, but to focus on the most important known pieces first. The iterative approach will naturally point to additional pieces that needed to be added and pieces that should be removed.

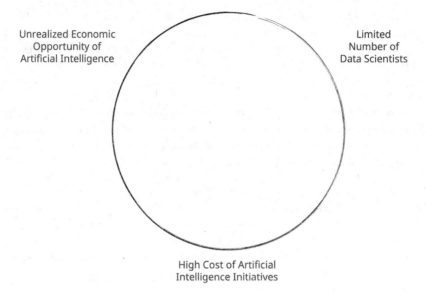

Unrealized Economic
Opportunity of
Artificial Intelligence

Limited
Number of
Data Scientists

High Cost of Artificial
Intelligence Initiatives

Figure 9.1   Connected Circle | 1

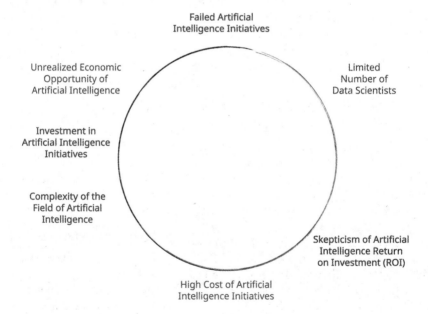

Failed Artificial
Intelligence Initiatives

Unrealized Economic
Opportunity of
Artificial Intelligence

Limited
Number of
Data Scientists

Investment in
Artificial Intelligence
Initiatives

Complexity of the
Field of Artificial
Intelligence

Skepticism of Artificial
Intelligence Return
on Investment (ROI)

High Cost of Artificial
Intelligence Initiatives

Figure 9.2   Connected Circle | 2

The unrealized economic opportunity of artificial intelligence leads to investment in artificial intelligence initiatives, some of which fail due to the complexity of the field of artificial intelligence, which leads to skepticism of the return on investment in artificial intelligence.

Figure 9.3 plots the interrelations between the various pieces. Failed artificial intelligence initiatives result in unrealized economic potential and in skepticism of the return on investment, which also leads to decreased investment and therefore further unrealized economic potential. The goal of this exercise is to build a model of the complex pieces and relationships between them within a system or network of systems. The elements around the circle that do not have arrows pointing to them are either immovable or require further examination. In the case of the field of artificial intelligence, although the complexity will not change, the accessibility will naturally evolve, which hints at additional elements that were not included in this diagram, such as data science bootcamps, open source frameworks, or low-code platforms, which are attempts by various organizations to solve this systemic challenge by replacing one of the pieces on the board or adding new pieces.

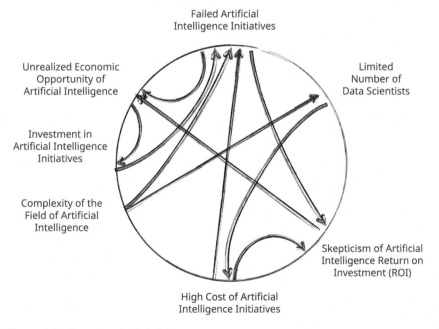

Figure 9.3   Connected Circle | 3

Elements or pieces around the circle that have many arrows pointing to them and/or stemming from them tend to be leverage points of the system. The next step in this exercise is replacing a leverage point with an alternative and mapping the change to the system. If, starting today, no artificial intelligence initiatives failed, the economic opportunity of artificial intelligence would start to be realized, skepticism of return on investment would reduce, and new elements would begin taking their place around the circle, such as successful artificial intelligence initiatives, which would add new product lines, which would lead to job growth, as illustrated in Figure 9.4.

While this example speaks to a market-wide network of systems, this process could be performed on internal organizational dynamics or even something as granular as team dynamics. The exercise of diagramming the connected circle around a given problem or market dynamic inevitably leads to ideation and highlights both risks and opportunities for leaders and managers to consider. In other words, this exercise draws attention to which pieces are on the board, which pieces are actively in play (or not), where the leverage points are, and to which degree the pieces are movable.

In connection to other frameworks in this book, this process can illuminate the complexity within a team, an organization, a market, or society, and

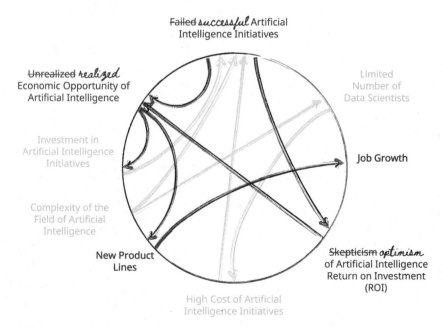

Figure 9.4   Connected Circle | 4

the pieces within that system, in tandem with analysis and synthesis to gain knowledge and understanding of those systems. The output of this exercise could be a future point from which the organization begins to develop a strategy with the organizational reasoning tree framework (see Chapter 15).

A Note for Individual Contributors

The above discussion is focused on how managers and leaders can see the whole system and adapt their perspectives to see the system of the organization and of the broader market(s) in which the organization exists.

This approach is also relevant for individual contributors, although the aperture is different. In my first corporate job, because I was new and untested, I was hired as a contractor to work in a data entry position. My position within the system was small, my understanding of the broader business and context even smaller, and the only measurement of my effectiveness in my position was how quickly I could enter data into the system while maintaining a consistent level of quality.

I started taking courses outside of my work hours to learn more about the underlying system we were using to see if I could add any additional value. I discovered a feature that allowed the automation of much of what our team was doing manually. I proposed to my manager that I could work on automating the most time-consuming workflows to enable the team to spend more time improving the quality of our work. Within a few months, I had worked my way out of a job, and less than six total months after joining the team on contract, I was hired as a full-time employee and assigned to my first consulting project.

If you are tempted to dismiss this example as "right place, right time," I will give you a second firsthand example, in which I was responsible for the analytics on a consulting project. Initially, I was working as an individual contributor. I released some descriptive and diagnostic analytics dashboards and, after positive client feedback, proposed several additions to my scope, including machine learning and process automation, for which I requested headcount. I was granted two headcount: one position mapped to business intelligence and one to machine learning. Together, we built a robust program that continued to receive positive feedback from our client.

Along the way, I became aware that we had 200 team members collaborating on a shared spreadsheet that, at the time, required checking out and checking back in, which meant that only one person could edit the file at a time. The function for which they were using the spreadsheet was simple, and I proposed to our project leadership that we build a lightweight software application to streamline the process, which, from a systemic vantage point, would create a platform that would fill a need in the broader market. My proposal was turned down, so I decided to teach myself software development and build it myself. Within a few months, it was deployed and we received positive feedback from the users and the client. I was then assigned a team of developers, and we began releasing new features every two weeks.

It all sounds straightforward and explainable in retrospect, but no one asked me to build more robust analytics, take on process automation, or look for opportunities to create a new product. Once I'd built up to the team of three and the client was happy with our work, I did not have to do anything about the 200 people sharing a spreadsheet, as it was not my team's issue. In fact, I was turned down when I proposed a path to resolving it. Looking at the whole system or set of systems can be a superpower in the hands of an individual contributor and create opportunities that otherwise would not exist.

Notes

1. The Henry Ford Museum of American Innovation, "Henry Ford and Anti-Semitism: A Complex Story," https://www.thehenryford.org/collections-and-research/digital-resources/popular-topics/henry-ford-and-anti-semitism-a-complex-story (accessed 7 January 2023).
2. https://github.com/Clover-Imaging-Group/AI4GoodVoicePicking.

CHAPTER 10

The Organization as a System

I n the educational system, disciplines are broken into their individual parts. Students major in marketing, accounting, or computer science. Achieving excellence in an individual discipline requires this approach. As important as excellence in a particular discipline, however, is an understanding of the interaction of that discipline with the rest of the organization.

I majored in music theory and composition, and had the honor of conducting choirs and orchestras during my studies. The performance of music within a group, whether a symphony orchestra, a choir, or a rock band, is inherently a systems discipline. If the best singer in the world is unable to blend their tone and volume with the rest of a choir, the result will be an uncomfortable listening experience. The same holds true for trumpet players, violinists, or any orchestral musician. They must master their individual instrument, and they must also master the skill of performing within the system of the orchestra.

Disneyland is one of the most elegant systems ever designed, delicately tuned to the creation of memorable, magical experiences for its guests. If everything about Disneyland remained the same, but the employees running the stores, restaurants, and rides all began behaving impatiently and impolitely toward guests, the system, and therefore the experience, would break down. If Disney tried to solve this problem by making tickets less expensive or investing in the creation of new rides, the system would continue to operate below its potential because the system requires high performance across the sum of its parts, and higher performance in a single part of the system cannot make up for low performance in another part of the system.

To further demonstrate the interconnectedness of systems, even the attempt to solve the problem by directly focusing on the employees presents a systems problem. Laying off the entire workforce to hire and train an entirely new set of employees, aside from the obvious misapplication of a mechanistic worldview in treating humans like replaceable machines, would result in backlash in the media and the expense of shutting down the park until the new workforce was hired and trained. Furthermore, replacing the workforce would not be the right solution if employee behavior changed due to a deficit in training or management programs, issues with shift lengths, or frustrations around wage. It would only be a matter of time before these conditions recreated challenges within the new workforce. The solution would be found within the interactions within these many interconnected parts of the system.

This requires a new form of leadership, evolved beyond the principles and habits of twentieth-century leadership, the conditions of which neither pursued nor welcomed empathy or feelings at work. In disentangling from a mechanistic worldview to a social systems worldview, the underlying motivation and belonging of the people who make up the broader system of an organization is a part of the system that cannot be overlooked. Fear was a powerful tool in past leadership regimes, but the social systems of the twenty-first century no longer accept fear as a motivating force. There are exceptions where fear continues to reign, usually in conjunction with fewer employment options, but the tolerance for command-and-control leadership has decreased in correlation to the increase of other employment opportunities and examples through the Internet.

Music provides a great analogy for this as well. If one could find a conductor who leads an orchestra through fear, and yet somehow manages to keep the players from leaving for other orchestras, those players, under fear of their leader, may play the correct notes at the perfect rhythm and at the right volume, but the music will ring hollow in the ears of the audience.

But the absence of fear is still not enough to lead a twenty-first century team or organization through a meaningful transformation or to retain or achieve a market leadership position. Great orchestral or choral conductors are not defined by their lack of poor leadership, but by their ability to inspire their people to each bring the best of themselves to the performance and to harmonize the group into a single unit (social system) on both a technical and emotional level.

Intraorganizational Systems

Leaders who successfully navigate the era of Autonomous Transformation to achieve meaningful market impact will be those who manage the interaction between the parts of the systems they oversee as well as the interaction with parts of the systems they do not oversee. At the C-level, this means managing the interactions between the organizations that fall within the leaders' purview *as well as* the interactions between those organizations and the organizations that do not fall within their purview. A chief technology officer could hire and develop the most talented technologists in the market, but if those technologists do not work well with the domain experts for whom they need to build technology solutions, the organization and the system have both failed.

This holds true at the vice president, general manager, director, and manager levels as well. Maintaining a strong business portfolio is an important contribution to the overarching organization, but ensuring the organization and its teams work cohesively with one another is equally important.

At the manager level, leadership begins with an understanding of each team member as an individual. What motivates them, what unique skills and experiences they bring to the team, how they do their best work, and where they feel belonging are starting points for understanding the person whose skills, decisions, and actions will contribute to the social systems of the team and the broader organization. This requires more effort than just getting to know each team member at a surface level, but it also affords managers the opportunity to better align work with the individual best suited to accomplish the outcome, based both on their skills as well as the role they play within the team and organization.

If a manager is presented with a request, for example, of the type that has always been routed to one particular team member, they may decide to follow the pattern for a number of reasons, such as the convenience of following a preexisting structure, the convenience of mutual understanding with that team member, or the known quality of that team member's output on that sort of task. Upon deeper understanding of the team, however, which is much more likely to be drawn out by an empathic manager than volunteered, it could be learned that the team member to whom that work is generally assigned has tired of the repetition of completing the same sort of task. This means that the quality is unlikely to improve and may even degrade with each new task of that nature assigned to that team member. Fortuitously, and not uncommonly for managers who are listening to their people, another team member may have confided in the manager that they are interested in learning more about the business and taking on challenging new tasks. Assigning the task to this team member, under guidance from the team member to whom the task had previously been assigned, creates the opportunity for a new degree of motivation and a new lens of experiences to be applied to the task. It also forms a new connection point between the two team members and engenders trust with the team member to whom the task has historically been assigned, and frees their bandwidth to focus on a new task or work stream, which they can approach with renewed vigor and interest.

Interorganizational Systems

In an interorganizational context, an issue could arise between individuals who report to different leaders. I once experienced this within a consulting organization. I was leading a technology practice, and my team consisted of consultants embedded on-site with clients. Through delivering great work and being in regular proximity with our clients, they were building strong, trusting relationships. One day, I got a message from one of our clients that a peer of mine from the business development and account management organization had scheduled time with her to discuss future projects. The client had taken the meeting, assuming the account management leader was planning to discuss opportunities to work with other practices within our firm since she was already working closely with our team. To her surprise, he wanted to spend the meeting scoping a roadmap of technology projects. When she asked if they could reschedule for a time that I or someone from my practice could join, he told her that I and my team were better focused on execution, and that he would be her partner in ideation.

Even if he had been an expert in technology, this overtly political move damaged our credibility with the client. In troubleshooting what had happened, I learned that it was systemic to our firm. Account managers received incentives for every deal for which they could demonstrate they made material contribution. My incentives were similar, but whoever "sparked" the deal would receive a much greater incentive.

The embedded nature of my practice meant that we would be first in line for sparking new deals without an intervention such as the one staged by my colleague. Furthermore, since we did not need his expertise to solution technology projects, no one had thought to include him in scoping, which meant he could not demonstrate material contribution to any of our extensions or new projects, and he was watching new deals, for which he had made the initial introductions, get booked in the system—deals for which he would not get compensated. Neither I nor my team were aware of this dynamic.

My motivation in approaching this problem was to discover what may have provoked my colleague's actions and resolve the issue as quickly as possible to ensure we did not lose business as a result of a lack of professionalism. Those with experience in consulting can relate to how quickly multiple millions of dollars of business can vanish with a slipup like this.

As frustrated as I was with my colleague's behavior, from a systemic perspective, I was not going to be able to solve the problem by focusing on his actions. He knew it was a risky move, but he was economically incented to try to find a way to inject his way into existing deals, and even more so to generate new deals.

Once I learned the full picture of the system, I could empathize with my colleague's motivations, although I still disagreed with his choices. I was able to understand the dilemma and frustration of leveraging one's cultivated network, introducing practice leaders, and seeing incentives decrease over time as practice leaders sold extensions and new projects. The system was imbalanced in favor of practice leaders, as account managers could not scope and close deals without practice managers.

Since we both knew the problem was going to affect our clients adversely, hurting long-term profitability for the whole firm, we brainstormed ways to resolve the systemic conflict of interests. Fortunately, we were able to find a solution we both agreed would be economically feasible for the firm and personally motivating for ourselves and our colleagues, and we presented the solution to our colleagues for their support. Together with their support, we approached our leadership team to propose the change, to which they agreed.

The change we proposed was focused on resolving the *interaction* between our two organizations when it came to selling new projects or project extensions, which would systemically remove the temptation for poor *actions*. Any sales that fell within an account covered by a given account manager would automatically contribute to that account manager's sales incentives, regardless of deal-by-deal involvement. Likewise, practice leader incentives shifted to focusing solely on billable hours within their practices. This removed the "meaningful contribution" clause, which meant we could divvy up efforts on sales pursuits based on whoever would be the most likely to land the deal with no economic incentive to compete with one other. In terms of the original client with whom this story began, my account management colleague was now paid for every new deal that my team landed, even if he had not heard about it until it was booked in the system. He was thus incented to recenter his focus on new deals and clients, which benefited his personal motivation as well as the whole system.

Industry-Specific Organizational Systems

Each industry has nuances to the way its organizations, systems, and ecosystems operate. In the financial sector, for example, there are no machine-filled factories. In oil and gas, technicians fly in helicopters to oil tankers in the ocean to repair systems that are not operating properly. In agriculture, there are hundreds of millions of acres of farmland that have no Internet or phone signal. In medicine, nurses and doctors combine science and kindness to heal wounds and diseases while endeavoring to create safe spaces to maintain patient dignity and mental wellbeing. In the utilities sector, technicians are assigned to travel around a state fixing and maintaining transformers and power lines. In the food industry, supply chain delays can mean wasting entire shipments of goods.

From a systems perspective, the interworkings of people, technological systems, business and legal policies, and the ecosystems that make up each industrial sector present a high degree of complexity, but fortunately they are not irreducibly complex when examined through a systems lens.

In the manufacturing sector, for example, the information and operational technology organizations are two distinct ecosystems serving distinct groups of manufacturing stakeholders with different (often opposing) incentives. The two organizations are supported by different software and system integration vendors, they have different buying behavior, and whereas information technology professionals make decisions informed by industry analysts, operational technology professionals have relationships with the original equipment manufacturers who make and maintain machinery in the plants, and they have to manage the additional consideration of unions, government, and regulatory bodies.

From an incentives and values perspective, information technologists are rewarded when they consolidate disparate systems, minimize the use of technology systems that are not reviewed and provisioned by the central information technology team, integrate manufacturing systems with enterprise systems, and ensure system-wide compliance and security. Operational technologists, on the other hand, are focused on leveraging technology to enable manufacturing plants to make production numbers; exceed quality, productivity, and cost targets; and improve safety.

A new project, stemming from either of these two organizations, is not going to intuitively fit neatly into the broader system when examining its parts. The disparity of the two groups, culturally, is well known in the manufacturing sector.

When we examine these groups through a systemic design lens, we can push past the obvious disparities and examine the system as a whole and the mutual benefit of improved interaction between these parts of the system. Manufacturers are able to invest further in new product lines and technologies when they are able to drive cost out of their processes. This is an outcome that would benefit the overarching system, and, therefore, executives from both the information and operational technology organizations.

The issue runs deeper, however, than any set of technological and business priorities—deeper than patching software to a system or instrumenting machinery. Those are only the first layer of considerations in a systems thinking examination of the situation.

Many in the field of manufacturing have a deep sense of cultural history and take pride in their work. In 1791, Alexander Hamilton delivered a report to the United States Congress entitled *Report on the Subject of Manufactures*, and argued the importance of removing reliance on British manufacturing. "Not only the wealth, but the independence and security of a country, appear to be materially connected to the prosperity of manufactures," he wrote.

Ensuing centuries provide evidence to the truth of this statement. The accumulation of the Industrial Revolution's expansion from Europe to the United States, Edison's creation of the first industrial research laboratory, and Ford's invention of the first assembly line fostered a national readiness for an unanticipated bolstering of manufacturing ensuing from the disruption of European manufacturing brought about by World War I. This boosted the U.S. economy from reliance on European exports to being the primary exporter worldwide. China has experienced a similar transformation, having transitioned from a developing, agrarian nation in the 1970s, when the United States' output was several hundred times that of China's, into an industrial powerhouse that produces nearly half of the world's industrial goods, overtaking the United States in global exports in 2010.

Another cultural element central to the manufacturing base is the act of creation. There is a physical, primal aspect to transforming raw elements into useful goods through the process of smelting, casting, crushing, cutting, or dyeing (to name a few).

Understanding the rich culture and history of an industry is a necessary input to the process of designing or redesigning systems within or to serve that industry. A lack of awareness or understanding of these factors is one of the primary reasons technologists and industry professionals have struggled to attain even a small proportion of their shared economic potential.

CHAPTER 11

Broken Systems

The Hedberg Strategy

Mitch Hedberg, a beloved comedian taken from the world too soon, once said, "If you find yourself lost in the woods, f%&! it, build a house. 'Well, I was lost but now I live here! I have severely improved my predicament.'"

Many of us have met organizational leaders who employ the Hedberg strategy. The combination of people, process, and systems in which they find themselves could be equated to being lost in the woods. Rather than work their way back out of the woods, they build a house. They grow comfortable with the lack of vision, the disjointed culture, and the poor quality of the results stemming from their team or organization. Then they decorate, trimming inefficiencies and adding incremental value from within a broken system. They may even get bonuses and promotions. The short-term loss from the employment of this strategy is wasted human and organizational potential. The long-term loss is the risk of the organization becoming defunct or reaching an existential crisis that requires a top-to-bottom redesign and restructuring of the whole organization.

A Broken System

The prevailing process by which most information or operational technologies intake projects from the rest of their organizations is focused on use cases and problems. This is then transformed into requirements that become the basis for finding an adequate vendor or designing and building a solution. When a given solution introduces a new problem, a new set of requirements to solve that problem are generated. The default trajectory of this process is incremental improvements on an existing system of ever-growing technical debt.

It should be noted that this process, with its emphasis on governance and streamlining, arose as a problem-solving response to the chaos experienced by most organizations in the early days of migrating from an analog to a digital world. When marketing analytics platforms, developed to understand viewership and engagement of an organization's website, first became available, in the absence of a process, marketing executives signed purchase orders or, more often than one would believe, used a corporate credit card, without the knowledge of the information technology organization. This behavior spread across organizations despite attempts to add processes for governance and streamlining. Even today, many business unit leaders choose to move forward on a vendor or solution while intentionally leaving their internal information technology colleagues out of the process entirely, or at a minimum, out of the procurement process. This takes place when they do not agree with the decision of their internal information technology organization or when they are not willing to wait for a formal review or procurement process.

Advisors who see this paradigm and its long-term implications face a moral dilemma when they know that their solution will solve a current problem (or use case) at the risk of detrimentally impacting the whole system in the future. They are incented to sell their solutions, not to solve a client's systemic trajectory. Additionally, the client is typically incented to report a specific, measurable impact (such as an increase in profitability) within the quarter or fiscal year, and is therefore likely to move forward with another vendor who is willing to propose a solution. The successful delivery of the project can then be used to secure more budget or be leveraged by the internal leader to get promoted, be granted additional headcount, or win an award.

On this last point, any systems-thinking-oriented advisor has undoubtedly run into this with their clients when they have defined a discrete problem they would like to solve, ideally within a certain time frame, and within their budget. When external advisors go through the process of pulling back the layers to ensure that the engagement will produce the best possible impact on the organization as a whole, and they identify that the problem the client has identified will not improve the performance of the broader system and that it would be best to include leaders from other organizations or to rescope the initiative, clients have reactions ranging from shock to rage to gratitude. The experience of shock and/or rage leads to less and less of this behavior except with clients with whom there is established trust.

Based on this history, the current iteration of the informational and operational technology project intake process is an improvement of the system. To any rational technology leader confronted with the obvious problem of each business unit making technological purchases without technological expertise or a system-wide view of the long-term implications, governance and process become the logical solution.

So why isn't it working?

It is a systems issue. The complexity of digital capabilities and advanced technologies have outgrown mechanistic processes and approaches, and a social systems approach is now needed. We are trying to improve on the current system without reexamining these organizations (information technology, operations technology, marketing, finance, etc.) as parts of a larger containing system.

That larger system exists to create value in a given sector at a pace that retains or expands its customer base and market competitiveness in order to sustain its ability to create value. Another layer upward shows that the organization exists within the broader system of the market, which has undergone a sweeping change, with looming disruptive forces, requiring the organization to accelerate its rate of value creation.

This understanding of the larger system, disaggregated back to an understanding of the subsystems within an organization, reveals the problem with the current structures and processes, which have not been designed with market competitiveness in mind, nor the broader organization's ability to create value in the market. Rather, the current structure and processes in most, but not all, organizations, is designed to maintain the current system.

Within this dynamic, innovative projects or new technologies discovered by business units become a threat to the stability of the existing system. The resultant adverse reaction in many organizations, unfortunately, has often increased the likelihood that business unit leaders create partnerships and sign agreements without consulting their internal counterparts.

One Reimagining of Internal Technology Organizations

To borrow from the story of Bell Labs earlier in this book (Chapter 6), if one were to design an organization from scratch today, given the understanding of the market just described and without any context of the existing organization, that design, along with other strategic priorities, would ensure that anything that provides "drag" to the speed of value creation is reimagined.

There are many ways this could be reimagined, the best of which would take into account both analysis of the existing organization, as well as synthesis of the broader market in which the organization creates value.

Counterintuitively, at first, the context of the technology market and ecosystem should also be considered, as information and operations technology organizations are not only a part of the system of their overarching organization or company, but are also a part within the system of the technology market and ecosystem, with whom they are competing for budget for technology projects, talent, and on whom they rely in order to create and maintain value.

When examining the broader technology market within which internal information and operations technology organizations are competing for projects from business units, there are two primary external competitors: consulting firms and product companies.

Consulting firms provide a rich repository of different structures, processes, and systemic design when examining how one might reimagine an internal technology organization.

An example of the difference between consulting firms and most modern organizations is that the structure of almost all consulting firms includes multiple reporting lines. At any given time, consultants are responsible to an account to which they have been assigned, a practice in which they are responsible for developing themselves as well as others, and whatever projects they have sold or to which they have been assigned. Incentives are aligned to delivering on existing projects, practice development, contribution to an account, and, depending on position, selling new projects.

In my own experience as a practice leader, my annual salary was broken into parts that relied on my ability to balance these priorities. I needed to find, attract, hire, retain, and grow the best talent in my practice areas while supporting sales discussions and providing attractive project proposals to clients to win the business and contribute margin to the firm while also maintaining consistent, quality delivery of existing projects to maintain client trust, gather case studies, and earn the right for future projects.

Put simply, my annual incentives would be reduced if my proposals were not the top proposals in a given procurement process, and even if they were, my incentives would be impacted if my team could not deliver the project at the right quality and within the budget that I had proposed. Furthermore, these were interdependent, as my ability to secure interesting and meaningful projects with clients was the basis of my ability to hire the best talent, which was the basis of my ability to secure and deliver projects.

Translating this example back into the context of reimagining internal technology organizations, if those organizations transitioned to "internal consulting firms," approaching the business units they supported as accounts, the technological areas in which they develop and maintain as practices, and (1) structured incentives based on the ability to deliver initiatives on time and at the right level of quality, and (2) structured their entire budgets on the basis of what initiatives they were able to win from their internal clients in a competitive bidding process.

Another rich insight from the field of consulting that could be applied to internal technology organizations is the idea of the bench. For those unfamiliar with the consulting industry, "the bench" is where consultants go in between project assignments. The bench exists in consulting because consultants can only bill to projects for which a project leader has budgeted a set of hours assigned to a specific task within the overall project plan. In other words, if there is not a need for a specific consultant on a project that could be justified to directly impact the margin of that project or an increase in spend from the client, that consultant is instead directed to the bench until they are able to secure their next project assignment.

"The bench" in consulting has two other important implications in the context of organizational reimagining. The first is the motivation the bench provides to consultants. Boutique firms typically do not pay consultants when they are on the bench. This is extremely motivating for consultants in terms of ongoing skill development as well as building deep relationships with clients and practice leaders. Being relegated to the bench means either that the market does not currently have a need for a consultant's skill set, that the consultant does not have the confidence of practice leaders or clients to deliver within that skill set, or that the firm is not able to gain client confidence in the firm's ability to deliver within that skill set. The first drives consultants to keep a razor-sharp perspective on the direction of the market and the ongoing development of their skills so as to secure assignments over other consultants. The second drives consultants to be rigorous in their delivery so as to foster and maintain confidence in their ability to deliver value within their domains. Even in organizations where there is a "paid bench," a low level of allocation or billable hours brings the risk of eventually being let go from the firm. In other words, the system of a consulting firm is designed in such a way that it is virtually impossible to "coast." Keeping one's job within a consulting firm requires constantly honing one's skills, ensuring exposure of those skills and delivery to leadership, and developing meaningful relationships.

On top of this, if a consultant does not exhibit high-quality work, the way most contracts are structured, the whole project could be canceled or the client can request that the consultant be dropped from the project, which would yield a severe blow to that consultant's career trajectory within that firm.

An examination of the typical modern internal technology organization, as a system, reveals a lack of these fundamental motivational drivers. Internal technology team members do not face the risk that, if their skills are deemed below the standards required by a business unit they support, they could be allocated to the bench and their salary or chargeability be dropped until they are reassigned. They also do not face the same risk that, if they deliver below expectations or fail to adequately maintain a positive relationship with their internal client, they could once again be relegated to the bench and not selected for future projects.

Likewise, most internal practice leaders, such as an internal software development leader, are not funded based on approved proposals for their internal counterparts, the successful project awards of which would be directly tied to their incentives and ability to maintain their practice. Instead, they generally serve as an internal bureaucracy, taxing business units regardless of the degree of the value they create.

One of the key systemic differences between internal technology organizations and an external consulting firm, which has no doubt been in the back of the mind of anyone from those organizations who is reading this chapter, is the need to develop and maintain the network of technological systems required for the overarching business and all of its functions to continue to create value. This is not a trivial task, and has historically been one of the key inhibitors of the reimagining of these functions.

There are many ways in which this aspect of the system could be addressed. For example, an committee for applied analysis and synthesis could be instilled to benchmark the competitiveness and performance of the network of technological systems against the backdrop of the broader market (like an internal Gartner or Forrester), and an element of each practice leader's incentives could be based on the health and performance of any aspects of the overarching system impacted by their practice throughout a given fiscal period. A corporate tax could continue to be maintained across the broader organization, but rather than funding the core headcount of the organization, it could be leveraged for building components of the network of systems that would improve the performance of the whole system and unlocking new horizontal capabilities that are irreducible and would not have been justifiable within the context of a single, vertical initiative.

This kind of internal transformation would also impact the overarching organization's approach to the ecosystem. This book dives deeper into ecosystems and the idea of "surprising and remarkable" partnerships later, but in the meantime, imagining a before/after paradigm of a conversation with a business unit leader, an internal technology organization, and an external consulting firm or product company illustrates the potential of this kind of reimagining.

Today, external organizations systematically target both internal technology organizations and business unit leaders, depending on their strategy and offerings. Meeting with a business unit leader without an internal technology counterpart is likely, and there is sometimes even a discussion on how to jointly navigate the internal technology process or team. Conversely, I have been told by account leaders that the chief information officer expressly instructed them, as external advisors, never to speak with business unit leaders without the presence of information technology team members. These are symptoms of this systemic issue, and not necessarily the fault of any one person, but, as my former boss at Underwriter's Laboratories would say, "It doesn't matter if it's our fault, it's our responsibility to fix it."

In the future of this reimagined scenario, because internal technology organizations share an incentive to ensure that the overarching organization delivers value at the speed necessary to retain and/or expand market share and market competitiveness, the idea of "shadow IT" could be eliminated almost overnight.

I recently spoke with a leader from a multibillion-dollar manufacturing company, in which new team members, when they are hired into their internal technology organization, go on a tour of the various groups the organization supports—not just to watch, but to participate. They spend a shift picking in the warehouse, taking customer calls, and assisting in manufacturing. This is a phenomenal method to generate understanding of what it takes to perform those jobs and would be great to see adopted more broadly. Taken a step further in the reimagining above, these team members could be incented based on business outcomes for the organizations they support. If a new team member not only takes customer calls to generate empathy and understanding of the experience of the internal customer support agents and customers, but does so with the knowledge that their incentives will be directly tied to metrics such as customer satisfaction (CSAT), average time to resolution, and net promoter score, this "skin-in-the-game" approach would pivot the orientation from reactive to proactive, driving team members to keep up with the latest technological advancements and methodologies for increasing customer satisfaction.

I saw this firsthand when I worked with a company whose product team created a subproduct team focused on improving the customer service experience. They built an entirely new suite of tools from the ground up to create the future of customer service that could not be supported by existing tools in the market, creating multiple capabilities that had not existed before. These technologists were coming up with extremely creative ideas and launching new software features to the customer service organization every two weeks. They treated the customer service agents like their end customers and they came to the table in each meeting with the customer service organizational leaders with their technological plans and ideas for tools they wanted to build and buy to improve the agent and end customer experience. It should be no surprise that this kind of internal partnership drove the net promoter score to an industry-leading number and customer service agents reported much higher job satisfaction than their peers within a different team in a different customer service team within the overarching organization.

In the case that an organization does not have the headcount to dedicate internal technology team members to individual lines of business, the outcome-based incentives could align to individual projects.

A Second Reimagining of Internal Technology Organizations

It was noted earlier that there are many possible reimaginings of internal technology organizations (as there are of any internal organization). Another reimagining is based on a second external force that competes with internal technology organizations for budget: product teams. These product teams are delivering new features to market at high speeds, are obsessed with their customers, and are focused on being easy to do business with. Examining product companies through the lens of analysis and synthesis yields a multitude of insights.

Product companies do not have practices as consulting firms do—they are organized by product. Each product typically has a vertically integrated team that includes all of the skills and capabilities required to build and maintain their product.

There are several different types of product companies: those focused on solving specific problems (point solutions), those focused on creating platforms for customers to solve their own problems (often with the help of consulting firms), and those focused on solving a suite of problems within a specific vertical domain.

Did you catch it? Even the way product companies are often described is in the context of problems. This thinking is so pervasive that it will take an intentional, focused effort to peel it back (if you are not reading this book linearly, I am referencing Chapter 6).

Ignoring the "problem" problem for now, synthesis thinking applied to product companies asks what role or function product companies serve in the broader system of the market. This can be observed through a thought experiment: imagining the market without any technology product companies. No Microsoft, no Apple, no Alphabet, no IBM, and so on. Imagine the path ahead if all of these companies and technology product companies as a category vanished overnight, and each individual organization was required to develop its own technologies to improve its ability to create value in the market. Every corporation would need to write its own software for spreadsheets and then build a team to maintain, add new features to, and debug that software, along with homegrown software applications for every imaginable function across the organization; the cost center for technology within the organization would skyrocket.

Technology product companies alleviate this need by providing solutions and capabilities to every organization at a fraction of the price it would cost them to develop and maintain it themselves. When Microsoft releases a new feature for Excel, whether it costs them a million or $200,000 to build, the cost only occurs once, and more than 30 million users around the world benefit from that new feature while continuing to only pay a monthly subscription fee as opposed to hiring and maintaining a spreadsheet software development team.

This approach is valuable for organizations not only from a cost perspective, but also from a feasibility perspective, as there is a limited number of advanced computer scientists in the world. When technology organizations incubate new products with a dozen or couple dozen researchers, that benefit is provided back to customers who may not have the resources or be able to source and retain the talent necessary to create that capability within their organization.

Disaggregating the function product companies play in the broader system of the market back down to insights that could inform the reimagining of internal technology organizations, product companies create value and are measured on their user base and subscription revenue.

If internal technology organizations were measured on usage and subscription revenue, an approach notably more experimental than the consulting-firm approach, business units could choose to unsubscribe from a service when they feel that the cost of that service does not justify the value it provides. This would mean bundling each service provided by the internal technology organization into a subscription price, which business unit organizations could weigh against subscriptions outside the organization. An important caveat to this approach is, because the entire stack would be vertically integrated, the subscription would almost inevitably be more than an external subscription. In order to ensure that the entire long-term picture is taken into account, external proposals should be weighed together with the implementation cost. I observed this mistake at a former organization, which ended up paying $65 million for the implementation of software that could have been built for less than $2 million and maintained for less than $500,000 per year.

This line of thinking begins to develop a hypothetical system that, now that a rough structure has been described, could be incrementally improved and examined from multiple angles until a clear picture has emerged and the organization can consider whether the proposed reimagination is both viable and the right direction to consider taking the organization.

A second line of thinking when considering the reimagination of internal technology organizations within the context of product companies through the lens of synthesis is whether product companies serve any other functions in the market beyond those previously examined. Cost savings and centralizing talent for solutions that impact a broad swath of organizations is critically important, but there is a limit to the function these companies can serve in this capacity, as the more domain-specific value created by a given product, the fewer overall customers they can serve.

This leaves a gap in the market, as the companies with the most revenue, and that can therefore offer the most competitive packages to secure top talent, are incented to create domain-agnostic software. The prevailing solution to this gap is a reliance on partners to directly build solutions on behalf of customers as well as intellectual property that can be leveraged to shorten the length of time it takes to implement a domain-specific project for future clients on the product company's platform.

The relevance of this paradigm for an organization in any industry other than technology is that if there is a need to build a new capability that does not yet exist in the market, is not simple enough to be a simple off-the-shelf solution from a platform company, and would therefore require a multimillion-dollar custom solution from a systems integrator, the organization would either be paying a premium on the system integrator's existing intellectual property, or would be funding that systems integrator's development of further intellectual property. There are cases in which either of these approaches is best for the organization. The case in which it would be worth considering an alternative approach is when the solution would be greatly applicable to many other organizations within the industry, and has yet to be developed due to the degree of domain expertise required. If the degree of required domain expertise aligns well to the core competencies of the organization, this solution could be developed in-house, with the plan to commercialize, funneling the profits back into the internal technology organization.

The goal of walking through these thought exercises together is not to provide specific recommendations for transforming internal technology organizations. Rather, it is to demonstrate the organizational context that leaders and managers must transform in order to effectively embark on an Autonomous Transformation journey. Each suborganization within a broader enterprise or organization can be similarly examined through the lens of the problem with solving problems and the negative effect system maintenance has had on the modern organization, and how the process of applying synthesis could be leveraged to reimagine an organization. This could be applied to any vertical or horizontal aspect of an organization once a desired future state of the organization has been determined, with the goal of ensuring organizational readiness, across the social system, to advance toward a more human future.

PART FIVE

Clear the Digital Fog

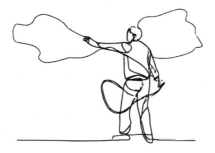

The fog of information can drive out knowledge.

—Daniel J. Boorstin

CHAPTER 12

Chaos, Noise, and Epistemology in the Digital Age

I n 1997, the most formidable chess player in the world was defeated by a machine in a six-game match. The world watched with bated breath as Garry Kasparov, who had held the title of world champion for 12 years, represented humankind against the machine. For those packed into the sold-out seats in the television studio and the millions of viewers who tuned into the matches at home,[1] this had little to do with computation, simulation, or pattern recognition. Because chess is considered both an art and a science, blending left and right brain thinking, it substituted as a match of human intelligence versus machine intelligence.

Thirteen years after *The Terminator* was released, an emblem of human genius had been conquered by machines.

Chaos, Noise, and the Three Logical Fallacies

That story and the form of its telling is familiar to many. The tempting takeaway is that machines have reached another critical milestone in catching up to human intelligence, but further examination reveals three fallacies commonly at play in this assumption.

First, the **slippery slope** fallacy: an argument in which a party asserts or assumes that a small first step leads to a chain of related events, culminating in some significant (usually negative) effect. There are those who raise this argument with each step technology takes in any direction.

But human consciousness is irreducibly complex. The path to recreating consciousness is not an accumulation of use cases or systems that can then be assembled into a human-like intelligence. The machine that beat Garry Kasparov (IBM's Deep Blue) took 12 years to develop, starting as a dissertation project by two researchers at Carnegie Mellon University in 1985, landing them both positions at IBM Research in 1989, where the team grew to six researchers who ultimately developed a machine with 32 processors that can analyze 200 million possible chess positions per second.[2] From a computer science perspective, this was a phenomenal breakthrough. This machine cannot, however, be combined with the machine that beat the world *Go* champion (DeepMind's AlphaGo) to stimulate consciousness, nor was it designed with that end in mind.

Second, a surprising number of people fall prey to the **non sequitur** fallacy when it comes to machines: an argument in which a conclusion does not follow logically from what precedes it.

When an article boasts of a machine's ability to analyze 200 million positions per second, or puts it in terms of how many years it would take a human to analyze the same number of positions, the non sequitur argument, boiled down to its simplest form, is: machines analyze chess positions faster than humans do; therefore machines can learn poetry and become conscious. An error remains even in the construct of this statement (beyond the obvious logical fallacy)—did you catch it? The use of the word "analyze" personifies the machine. Put more precisely and simply: machines apply math or logic programmed by humans faster than humans do; therefore machines can learn poetry and become conscious.

The ability to perform mathematical calculations at lightning speed, weighing probable outcomes based on a predetermined list of objectives and rules set by human experts, is impressive and useful, but it does not mean that the machine understands chess, nor can it venture beyond chess to any other pool of knowledge, any more than a fast calculator can understand the underlying concept of the oranges divided among friends in a math problem, let alone the concepts of friends or the classroom.

Third, the **appeal to authority** fallacy: the argument that if a credible source believes something, then it must be true.

This is a tricky topic because some of the voices that have spoken publicly about their concerns with regard to the development of artificial intelligence are regarded as heroes, and have deep credibility in their respective fields. The fog of confusion that often surrounds press about statements from these industry or academic leaders can be lifted with two questions.

First, what did they actually say?

Second, what is their field of expertise?

On December 2, 2014, the British Broadcasting Corporation (BBC) released an article titled: "Stephen Hawking Warns Artificial Intelligence Could End Mankind." The online post included a five-minute snippet of an interview with Professor Stephen Hawking, one of Britain's preeminent scientists, transcribed as follows:

INTERVIEWER (RORY CELLAN-JONES):   When you watch software engineers and machine learning experts at work as they have been on this project, how far along the path to artificial intelligence do you think we are?

STEPHEN HAWKING: The primitive forms of artificial intelligence we already have, have proved very useful. But I think the development of full artificial intelligence could spell the end of the human race. Once humans develop artificial intelligence, it would take off on its own, and redesign itself at an ever increasing rate. Humans, who are limited by slow biological evolution, couldn't compete and would be superseded.[3]

Within hours, dozens of articles were released by reputable journalists from established media outlets. Here are some of their titles and first lines:

- "Does Rampant AI Threaten Humanity?," BBC News
  "Pity the poor meat bags."[4]

- "'Artificial Intelligence Could Spell End of Human Race' – Stephen Hawking," *The Guardian*
  "Technology will eventually become self-aware and supersede humanity, says astrophysicist."[5]

- "5 Very Smart People Who Think Artificial Intelligence Could Bring the Apocalypse," *Time*
  "On the list of doomsday scenarios that could wipe out the human race, super-smart killer robots rate pretty high in the public consciousness."[6]

- "Beware the Robots, Says Hawking," *Forbes*
  "British physicist Stephen Hawking has warned of the apocalyptic threat artificial intelligence (AI) poses to people[. . .]"[7]

- "Sure, Artificial Intelligence May End Our World, But That Is Not the Main Problem," *Wired*
  "The robots will rise, we're told. The machines will assume control. For decades we have heard these warnings and fears about artificial intelligence taking over and ending humankind."[8]

Those are some heavy titles, which undoubtedly received a significant degree of attention. The goal of sharing these examples is not to address or change the media, but to equip individuals to find the signal in the noise, which requires returning to what Professor Hawking actually said: "I think the development of full artificial intelligence could spell the end of the human race. Once humans develop artificial intelligence, it would take off on its own [. . .]." There are three important qualifiers in his statement: "full," "could," and "would." Full artificial intelligence is used interchangeably with artificial general intelligence, defined as a machine capable of understanding the world as well as any human, and with the same capacity to learn how to carry out any range of tasks without any additional programming. As of this writing, this kind of system does not exist, nor would the number of researchers and technological breakthroughs required as a predecessor be economically viable. Professor Hawking is speaking of a theoretical situation, as indicated by the use of "could" and "would," in which the development of full artificial intelligence *could* spell the end of the human race, as the artificial intelligence *would* take off on its own.

Having answered the question "What did they actually say?," the second question is "What is their field of expertise?" If the foremost leader in chemical engineering made a prediction about artificial intelligence, it would be easy, though misguided, to generalize credibility from their field of expertise to the field of computer science, and vice versa. This is not to say that the prediction would inherently be incorrect, but that more digging is required and the prediction should not be taken at face value, particularly when it comes to an existential topic.

Epistemology in the Digital Age

Michelangelo Buonarroti's quotation, "I saw the angel in the marble and carved until I set him free," is surprisingly applicable to the discussion of humans and machines. If a person's mental picture of a given topic, such as artificial intelligence, begins as a block of marble, an article title alone can be enough to chisel into the stone. A conversation with a colleague, a movie or television show, another article, a rumor about a project at work, a post on social media—as these accumulate, a rough shape begins to emerge. This becomes dangerous when decisions are made based on these rough sketches, especially if each attempt to chisel into the marble is not closely examined.

There are two methods by which to examine inbound information. The first is through **zooming out to the whole picture**. Returning to the story of Garry Kasparov and Deep Blue, there is another side of the picture that can be illuminated in asking why IBM would invest in an eight-year journey with six researchers to beat a human at chess. The answer? To build and demonstrate computing capability. Put another way: to create more products, improve existing products, gain visibility, and deepen credibility.

IBM did this again with *Jeopardy* in 2011,[9] and this approach has become an established marketing tactic for technology companies, as it is an engaging way to demonstrate meaningful technological breakthroughs. In 2013, DeepMind built and demonstrated their breakthroughs in reinforcement learning by creating a model that surpassed human expert abilities on Atari games, and they created a computer program (AlphaGo) that beat the *Go* world champion in 2015.[10] The important takeaway is that these are not a part of a cohesive, coordinated advancement of artificial intelligence toward the goal of the singularity, as is often imagined or misinterpreted. Rather, corporations, academics, and research institutes are economically and reputationally incented to demonstrate the power of their platforms and research breakthroughs in memorable ways.

A second application of zooming out to the whole picture can be found in the current state of the life cycle of research, as visualized in Figure 12.1. Research almost always begins with a question of capability. Can a machine consistently beat a human at chess? Can a machine be used to detect cancer? Can a system be created that can accurately detect a spill in a manufacturing plan?

Once the scope of the research has been defined, the researchers then need to secure funding, whether through grants from governments, nonprofits, business partners, or, in the case of corporate researchers, from a central funding entity and/or business units who hope to apply the research to their business.

The eureka moment can arrive within months, after 12 years as in the case of Deep Blue, or it may never come. Leadership in research requires the agility to scrap and learn from research when it becomes clear that it is not feasible or viable to continue pursuing it, as well as the inverse: the resilience to continue funding research against uncertainty.

After the eureka moment, with documented certainty that the breakthrough is repeatable and demonstrable, an academic paper is written and submitted to a peer-reviewed publication.—in this case, "The Application of Machines in the Elevation of Brobdingnagian Materials," or "Using Machines

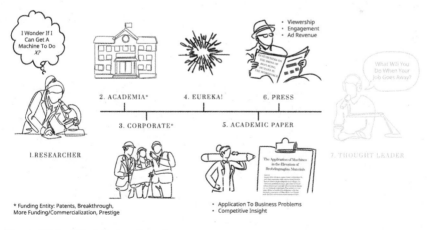

Figure 12.1   What Researchers See

to Lift Heavy Things." For the sake of this example, it would be fair to assume that the researchers, as is commonly observed, speak to potential applications of their research in industry, such as "This type of technology could contribute to human safety in manufacturing and warehousing environments by reducing the need for humans to lift objects greater than 50 pounds."

From here, the research can take one or more of five paths, without consistent correlation to the quality of the research:

Path 1: Business leaders endeavor to apply the research to real-world applications and succeed.

Path 2: Business leaders endeavor to apply the research to real-world applications and fail.

Path 3: Journalists write compelling, accurate accounts of the research.

Path 4: Journalists write compelling, inaccurate accounts of the research.

Path 5: The academic paper lives on in archives, but is neither discussed nor applied more broadly.

Some research travels concurrently down Paths 1–4. Others, such as in Figure 12.2, jump immediately to Path 4. Thought leaders subscribing to those media channels to gather content for potential posts may or may not see the original academic paper. It is therefore up to readers to dig deeper before allowing an attention-grabbing post or article to influence their perception of a topic.

The second method by which to examine inbound information is through the lens of **economic incentive**. In the next chapter, we discuss

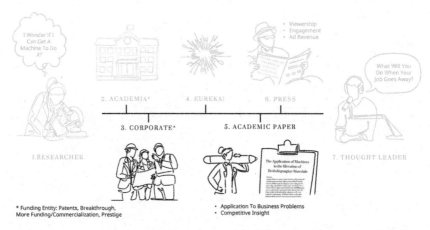

Figure 12.2 What Business Leaders See

testing economic incentives in business and advisory relationships, but for the purpose of navigating noise and chaos as it pertains to announcements, press releases, news articles, and posts online, the evaluation of economic incentive is critical to ascertaining the validity of the information.

Consider, for example, if a professor at a prestigious institution were to write a paper titled "Why We Need to Stop Investing in Artificial Intelligence Research Immediately."

Now consider if a vice president at a traditional automation company had written the paper instead.

How about an independent thought leader and keynote speaker?

When it is laid out as above, it becomes fairly clear where economic incentives intertwine with the message, regardless of its validity.

The vice president, for example, may be writing the paper in an effort to thwart research in a technology that is undermining the traditional automation business.

The thought leader may have chosen that title due to its stickiness, and pivot from the dogmatic title to a more general discussion about investments in artificial intelligence research, review trends, and end with a rhetorical question or call to action.

The professor is compelling because, depending on their position at the institution, they would either have no incentive to write such a paper, or there may even be a disincentive, which increases the likelihood that the professor truly believes in the premise of the paper.

Zooming out to see the whole picture in combination with the lens of economic incentive is the first step in gaining clarity amidst the sea of fog that has enveloped organizations and society in the digital age.

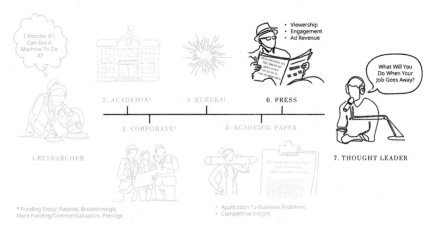

Figure 12.3   What the Average Professional Sees

These concepts and frameworks apply to the required evolution of epistemology in the digital era. Mastering the art of epistemology will be a key factor for effective leadership, as well as on the personal level, for ensuring that one is considering the correct existential questions in developing and maintaining a sense of self in the context of the human–machine paradigm. Epistemology, as defined by Merriam-Webster's dictionary, is "the study or a theory of the nature and grounds of knowledge especially with reference to its limits and validity."[11] As philosophers tend to prefer (also much easier to remember), epistemology can be summarized as "How do you know that you know what you know?"

Reviewing each new piece of information or perspective, be it an article, a conversation, a book, or a meeting, and determining whether the three logical fallacies are at play, zooming out to the whole picture, and examining the economic incentive of the source of the information and of the subjects (both individuals and organizations) will increase confidence and clarity in what you know and whom to trust.

Notes

1. IBM, "Deep Blue," IBM's 100 Icons of Progress, https://www.ibm.com/ibm/history/ibm100/us/en/icons/deepblue (accessed November 17, 2022).
2. Ibid.
3. R. Cellan-Jones "Stephen Hawking Warns Artificial Intelligence Could End Mankind," BBC News, December 2, 2014, https://www.bbc.com/news/technology-30290540 (accessed September 12, 2022).
4. W. Ward, "Does Rampant AI Threaten Humanity?," BBC News, December 2, 2014, https://www.bbc.com/news/technology-30293863 (accessed September 12, 2022).
5. S. Clark, "Artificial Intelligence Could Spell End of Human Race: Stephen Hawking," *The Guardian*, December 2, 2014, https://www.theguardian.com/science/2014/dec/02/stephen-hawking-intel-communication-system-astrophysicist-software-predictive-text-type (accessed September 12, 2022).
6. V. Luckerson, "5 Very Smart People Who Think Artificial Intelligence Could Bring the Apocalypse," *Time*, December 2, 2014, https://time.com/3614349/artificial-intelligence-singularity-stephen-hawking-elon-musk/ (accessed September 12, 2022).
7. P. Rodgers, "Beware the Robots, Says Hawking," *Forbes*, December 2, 2014, https://www.forbes.com/sites/paulrodgers/2014/12/03/computers-will-destroy-humanity-warns-stephen-hawking/ (accessed September 12, 2022).
8. M. Coeckelbergh, "Sure, Artificial Intelligence May End Our World, But That Is Not the Main Problem," *Wired*, December 4, 2014, https://www.wired.com/2014/12/armageddon-is-not-the-ai-problem/ (accessed September 12, 2022).
9. IBM, "Deep Blue."
10. DeepMind, AlphaGo, https://www.deepmind.com/research/highlighted-research/alphago (accessed November 17, 2022).
11. "Epistemology," Merriam-Webster dictionary, https://www.merriam-webster.com/dictionary/epistemology.

CHAPTER 13

Silicon Valley, Wall Street, and the Factory Floor

Our society faces an unprecedented degree of division. The first quarter of the twenty-first century has seen industries turned upside down, the creation of new markets, new social and class structures, a dramatic shift in the day-to-day human experience, and increased economic imbalance.

It is surprising to remember or believe that in 1997, the domain "google .com" was registered, Netflix was founded, smartphones did not exist, and the percentage of personal computer ownership in the United States was only 35%.[1]

The Divide Within

If organizational functions were categorized into the most simplified buckets, they would be technology, business, and industry. Many individuals span more than one of these buckets, especially as they move into leadership positions, but it's important to draw this distinction because it provides a taxonomy for examining the divide within organizations that has taken place in the first quarter of the twenty-first century.

One of the earliest social shifts has been the transition of technology professionals from the back office to the boardroom and into leadership positions throughout companies. The mandate for every business to become a digital business lest it go the way of Blockbuster has led to this shift in decision-making power. This has been and remains a profound cultural shift. IT leaders have transitioned from *supporting* business functions, setting up intranets and maintaining computer hardware and software, to *informing* business decisions, advising which Internet hosting service should be purchased to create the organization's website and whether the organization's inventory can be converted to a database, to *leading* board-level agenda items: organization-wide digital transformation or new digital lines of services or products.

If we look back further than 1997, we observe a similar shift in the decision-making power transitioning from industry leaders to business leaders in a repeated cycle on a micro level, and on a macro level in the twentieth century as business leadership rose to an elite profession due to the influence of the world wars and the Depression.

Artifacts of these dissenting factions can be found today, some of which are quite obvious. Shadow IT is a chief example, as it gives business and industry leaders control over their technology choices, spend, and implementations. Regrettably, it damages the broader system of the organization. Disagreements about building-versus-buying capability is another example of these misalignments. One firm I worked with was deep into the due diligence process of a proposed several-hundred-million-dollar acquisition when the question was raised as to whether a "build" assessment had been run on the underlying technology. It had not been considered. The business leaders wanted the capability as soon as possible, and were willing to spend almost 100 times more (the analysis ended up revealing this cost differential) to buy the capability than to bring their internal technology organization into the discussion.

A further divide between these disciplines (business, technology, and industry) arose when some technologists realized they could speak the language of technology any time they wanted to skirt a business conversation or, worse, mislead business and industry leaders.

In Figure 13.1, you can see the juxtapositions of these factions at their best and at their worst. At their best, technologists understand that their technological capabilities are only as valuable as the business models and domain expertise with which they are paired.

The economic potential when leaders can balance this equation across organizations is exponential.

An imbalance in the equation is found when organizations are operating at their worst: disrespecting one another's expertise, making decisions in silos, and holding back the organization's ability to create value and make meaningful impact. This is unsustainable from both a profit and a culture perspective, tipping the organization into a nosedive.

AT THEIR WORST   AT THEIR BEST

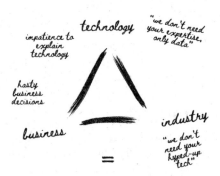
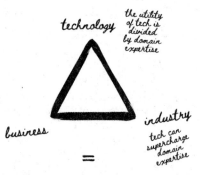

TOXIC CULTURE,   MORE MEANINGFUL WORK,
UNSUSTAINABLE BUSINESS   MORE JOBS, MORE VALUE

Figure 13.1   The Division of Expertise

The Divide Across

The View from One Side of the Field

The technology consulting and technology industries are home to an immense amount of technological capability. These organizations face a different set of challenges than those outlined in the previous section as there is a natural alignment and orientation toward technology across technology, business, and industry leaders because the industry is also technology. The greatest challenge arises when these organizations approach other industries in attempts to partner or to sell software and/or services.

When a consultant or software professional approaches an organization outside their industry, the first two decisions they must make are at which altitude should they start the conversation, and whether to approach the technology, business, or industry organization within their target client. Both come with trade-offs and are influenced by factors such as the applicability of the technology, existing relationships, and balance of trade.

Consultants and software professionals are often instructed by the chief information officer (CIO) or someone in the CIO's organization, for example, to never hold a discussion with business or industry leaders in the organization without members of the information technology organization present. From a balance of trade perspective, if the information technology organization is spending tens of millions of dollars on a managed service or software licensing, it may not matter how applicable the technology could be to another organization or where there may be existing relationships.

Alternatively, if a new relationship is budding between a software advisor and an industry leader, the software advisor may be advised not to connect with or consult with the information technology organization.

Both of these behaviors are harmful to the overarching organization and can be difficult for software and advisory leaders to navigate.

The View from the Other Side of the Field

Most business and industry leaders have a handful of technological advisors they trust internally and externally. When the technology, business, or industry evolves past the capabilities of those advisors, however, or in the case of attrition, how do you find the right next advisors?

The rift between the technology, business, and industry factions becomes even more apparent and problematic in this scenario, where the technology organization is external to the business and therefore does not share the same fiscal incentive to ensure success.

This is compounded by the misdeeds of some technology advisors, motivated by short-term gain or attempting to overcome a lack of expertise. Any technology advisor attempting to build relationships with new potential clients must first undergo pressure testing to demonstrate both credibility and trustworthiness, and rightfully so. Technology's ability to create value is equal to its ability to create harm. Thankfully, the majority of failed projects stop at having wasted resources, tossed aside once it becomes clear that the solution will not solve the problem for which it was being developed or implemented. Regrettably, these instances further deepen the wedge between technology, business, and industry leaders.

If you are a business or industry leader, you are likely inundated with messages from technology advisors asking for 10 minutes of your time to share a demonstration of their software, a discussion of their capabilities, or to discuss your needs. The painful truth for many in this position, beyond the lack of trust at the starting line, is the lack of time and resources to sufficiently vet each individual salesperson, technological capability, or solution. The test shown in Figure 13.2 can be leveraged to aid in navigating new relationships with technology advisors.

The Economic Incentive Test (Figure 13.2) can illuminate the trustworthiness of an advisor or salesperson before any meetings take place, and requires only three steps:

1. Give the advisor five disparate problem statements.
2. Plot the advisor's recommendations on the graph.
3. Do the math.

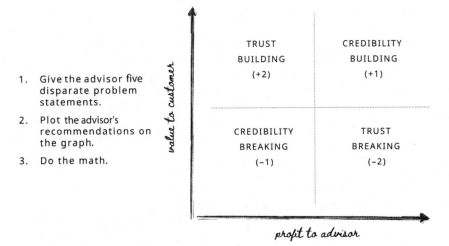

1. Give the advisor five disparate problem statements.
2. Plot the advisor's recommendations on the graph.
3. Do the math.

Figure 13.2   The Economic Incentive Test

Creating five problem statements should be relatively simple for any business or industry leader. The key for this test to yield results is to make sure the statements are disparate or diversified enough that most technology solutions cannot and should not be able to solve them all. This provides an opportunity to see how the advisor or salesperson handles the problem statements for which their technology is not a fit. If, for example, they zero in on the single problem statement for which their technology is applicable, ignoring the rest, that is a different kind of approach than an advisor who acknowledges that they can only help you with one, but they have industry contacts or others within their company to whom they could introduce you to look into addressing the other four. The quality and applicability of those recommended additional contacts and their related products and/or services also speaks to the advisor's credibility. The difference highlighted in this example is approaching the relationship in a transactional capacity, where a salesperson is only listening for use cases for which there is a sales opportunity, as opposed to approaching the relationship in an advisory capacity, focused on adding value beyond individual sales opportunities. You will thank yourself down the road for making this distinction upfront.

A fictional example illustrates this test in action:

Wei is a leader at a large manufacturing company. She is approached by Anders, who works for a consulting firm. Anders reaches out to Wei, requesting time to make introductions and to learn more about what challenges Wei's organization may be facing. Wei replies that she appreciates Anders' reaching out, that she does not have a lot of time to meet, but she would be interested in Anders' perspective on five challenges her organization is looking at solving in the near future, the details of which she shares in an attachment. Anders replies after two business days and shares a document containing proposed solutions, with documented assumptions and questions that need validation, to three of the problem statements. In his note, he calls out that his practice does not focus on the other two problem areas, but that he has a colleague who he believes could be helpful in addressing them, if Wei does not mind his making an introduction and sharing details with them.

In the presentation, Anders shares details on how his practice would approach the three applicable problem statements, but that he believes they should start with the solution (pictured in the "Trust Building" square of Figure 13.3) where Wei's organization will realize the most value with the lowest initial cost. According to the grid shown in the figure, this is a trust-building proposition. Anders could have skipped that problem statement or reordered it behind a problem statement that would have secured him a higher initial deal size. His choice is a signal of trustworthiness. Whether the solution is correct or the technology is sound must still be vetted, but at this stage, the recommended starting point and the fact that all three proposed solutions score positively in the test (with a total score of 4), Wei can trust that the advisor is choosing a trustworthy sales and partnership approach.

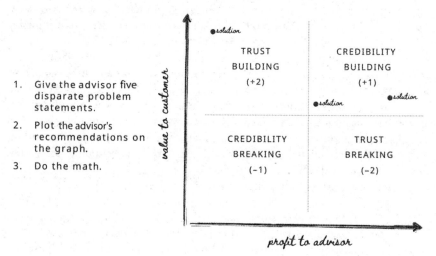

1. Give the advisor five disparate problem statements.

2. Plot the advisor's recommendations on the graph.

3. Do the math.

Figure 13.3   The Economic Incentive Test (Plotted)

If you begin using this test, you will see thresholds begin to emerge and, as you take risks on new technology and/or consulting partners, tracking their long-term credibility and trustworthiness back to how they initially scored on this graph will inform whether you should consider raising or lowering your threshold.

If you are a technology sales director or managing partner at a consulting firm, you can use this test in interviewing and training new hires, as well as reviewing proposals of team members to measure and improve their projected credibility and trustworthiness over time.

This test is a starting point in taking extra steps to carefully examine our own credibility and the credibility of those approaching us with solutions to begin closing the divide across organizations.

The Divide Without

Our world is faced with social tensions between classes and geographies. These have been exacerbated by the economic imbalance created by the past several decades of technology growth. The underlying issues range from unequal access to opportunity to bias in the application of technology, the creation of an entire market focused on extending screen time, the shifting of classes in favor of those working in the technology industry, and outright unethical practices (to name a few).

Resolving these societal, systemic issues is a moral obligation on an individual level. Unfortunately, individual moral obligation has often been demonstrated to be insufficient to drive change through a system, much less a network of systems. Demonstrating positive influence on the business, however, can be and has been leveraged to generate organizational and societal momentum.

The digital divide, first revealed by the United States Department of Commerce in 1995, has a direct correlation to organizations now and in the future. The system in which an organization physically exists contains talent pools and long-term talent pipelines. Addressing the digital divide in the local communities in which an organization operates benefits the long-term continuity of the organization due to the development of local talent. It also has implications on attracting and retaining talent, and positively influencing the organizational culture with meaning and belonging.

Seattle is a great example of this. Known as the cloud capital of the world, the "system" of Seattle currently includes Amazon, Boeing, Microsoft, Nordstrom, SAP Concur, Expedia, multiple offices for Google, Meta, SalesForce, Tableau, and a host of other businesses.

A child growing up in Seattle today is highly likely to meet someone who works at one of these companies, go to school with children of employees of these companies, have access to a computer or tablet at a young age (provisioned by the school), have STEM options before, during, or after school, and have a clear understanding of what it would be like to have a job in the technology industry.

In contrast, a child growing up in a town with less organizational presence will need intervention to experience the benefits of the virtuous cycles that exist in cities like Seattle. Some of these interventions (the provisioning of devices and STEAM educational opportunities) can be funded by governmental education systems, but organizations that exist within the system have a symbiotic opportunity to lend their resources to contribute to the social good and to ensuring there is a steady flow of local talent development for the future.

Note

1. U.S. Department of Labor, Bureau of Labor Statistics, "Computer Ownership Up Sharply in the 1990s," *Issues in Labor Statistics* 99-4 (1999).

CHAPTER 14

The Multiplication of Expertise: A Leadership Imperative

Clearing the fog around nascent technologies, such as artificial intelligence, the Internet of Things, digital twins/simulations, robotics, and virtual and augmented reality, has proven to be an insurmountable challenge for most organizations. This is part of the reason only 13% of data science projects make it into production.

Each of these terms has reached a degree of semantic satiation, the psychological phenomenon in which repetition causes a word or phrase to temporarily lose meaning for the listener, who then perceives the speech as repeated meaningless sounds.[1] Moreover, many conversations begin with the assumption that there is a shared understanding of the definition of a given technology, when it is more likely that that is not the case.

If five people sit down in a conference room to discuss artificial intelligence, for example, setting aside each individual's emotional sentiment regarding their idea of the technology, their understanding of its inner workings and application will almost necessarily vary.

Because uncertainty registers as pain in the brain, as discussed earlier in this book, and leads to further confusion, lack of clarity is one of the greatest threats to an organization and it is the responsibility of leaders to push through this uncertainty until clarity and mutual understanding is reached.

But how?

Asking technologists to "dumb it down" damages the dignity of industry and business team members. The same holds true in the opposite direction when industry or business leaders pontificate on the finer points of theory regarding their domains of expertise.

Imagine if you gathered the top experts (on anything) from three different countries in a room, and they all spoke different languages with no overlap.

The latent potential would be obvious. This phenomenon happens on a daily basis in organizations around the world, where professionals are fluent in the language of business, technology, and industry, but not necessarily in the adjacent languages, despite the fact that they share a common oral and written language.

As illustrated in Figure 14.1, these experts are capable of finding a shared language, but it requires intentionality and, more often than not, facilitation. Fluency in more than one of these languages is often a key differentiator that leads to leadership opportunities, as many leaders can attest.

But personal fluency is not enough. It benefits decisions a leader will make and provides the ability to give meaningful feedback across verticals, but the ability to foster and facilitate discussions between these groups is far more powerful.

Esther is a business leader at a chemical organization, and when she was notified that a supplier was increasing its prices on a raw material, she looked into which products used that material and analyzed the projected profitability of each product given the increased expense. She found that several products retained solid margins and therefore required no immediate action, but one

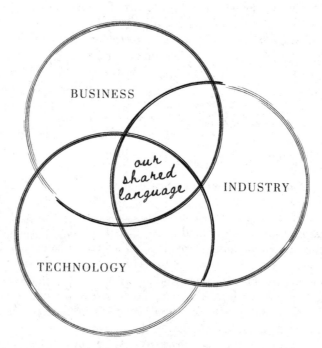

Figure 14.1   Finding a Shared Language Across Domains of Expertise

product in particular was no longer profitable with the increased expense. She analyzed various scenarios and determined that a 2% cost reduction would render the product sufficiently profitable.[2]

How she approaches the industry leader now that she has this information is critical. Which would you choose?

[ ] "You need to find a way to cut costs by 2% on the Product X line or we're going to have to shut it down."

[ ] "Our supplier for Chemical X just raised their prices, putting Product X's profitability at risk. I ran an analysis, and we'll be able to absorb the price increase if we can find a way to drive 2% cost out of production."

[ ] "The economics of Product X are no longer viable. It's now the lowest performer in our product line, and only a 2% reduction in cost can save it from the chopping block."

The answer is obvious when the options are presented side by side, but the first and third options are still taking place daily all over the world. These approaches can be motivated by a desire to create urgency, a desire to wield power ("I have the power to shut a portion of your business down"), or they could be a result of moving too quickly and not thinking through the impact of one's communication.

There are three points to note about the second communication: Esther did not overload the communication with irrelevant specifics (how much the prices were raised or how profitable Product X is); she summarized the business analysis and translated it into the industry leader's context (she didn't mention the specific type of analyses she used, which platform she used, how many data points she analyzed, or with whom she verified the findings of the analysis); and she used inclusive language, indicating a shared problem and mutual need to find a solution.

Philippe is the industry leader at the chemical organization responsible for Product X, who has received Esther's communication. He and his team take pride in the fact that Product X is the most unique chemical formulation in the organization, and he is personally connected to the formulation, as it is based on research he performed during his PhD studies. Over the past 20 years, they have built a strong team, fine-tuning the formulation for the existing product and the systems and processes to drive cost out of production. Due to the influx of competition over the decades since product launch and its effect on pricing and profitability, Philippe has begun testing a hypothesis of a slightly different formulation and the potential for the development of a subsequent, more powerful product that would once again differentiate the organization in the market.

Esther's message posed three key challenges for Philippe (beyond his personal tie to the product). First, the chemical formulation is highly sensitive, leaving little room for experimentation due to the risk of significant waste or even disaster. Second, because the product will be rendered obsolete within a year if he can complete his research, he does not want to invest time and expertise in further fine-tuning the process. Third, his team does not have the appetite for another optimization project.

Unfortunately, none of this context changes the problem for a business leader who has to account for specific margins within a quarter or fiscal year.

Philippe hits "reply" on Esther's email and drafts three responses. Which would you choose?

[ ] "Product X put this organization on the map. You'll have to find a way to cut costs out of the business processes to account for this or take the loss until we can launch the next iteration of the product."

[ ] "There is a nuance and precision to the production process for which I feel like the right robotic capabilities could be applied to increase yield and reduce waste. When we surveyed vendors a few years ago, they hadn't gotten the cost-to-value equation quite to where we needed it to be, but I will revisit those discussions to see where things stand today."

[ ] "Supplier X has been increasing their prices arbitrarily since we started working with them. Let's start the process of exploring other suppliers to see if we can get the profitability equation back to where it should be."

In this case, the second and third answers would both be valid. Philippe resisted the temptation to overload the communication with irrelevant specifics, such as the nuances of the production process or the chemical properties and potential reactions, and instead translated into Esther's context as a business leader and employed inclusive language.

Mia is a technology leader and peer to Esther and Philippe. Philippe adds her to the email thread with Esther and asks if she and her team can assist in facilitating discussions with robotics vendors and if they might be able to first qualify the potential vendors. He shares the documentation from previous vendor discussions and the requirements that were gathered at the time with a callout that some of the specifics have changed, but the information is directionally correct.

Mia leads a technology organization that includes technical resources such as technical architects, software developers, user experience designers, data analysts, data scientists, machine learning engineers, and database administrators. Since joining the organization less than a year ago, her focus has been on establishing a hybrid cloud strategy, migrating and modernizing applications, and removing reliance on third-party vendors in favor of a build-first strategy.

Philippe's team has the highest reliance on third-party vendors in the organization, and Mia and her team have been acutely interested in updating and standardizing the technology supporting his product line. In reading Philippe's email, Mia sees an opportunity to map the current state and paint a vision for the efficiencies that could be gained from streamlining regardless of whether robotics can be built into the process. Mia drafts three responses; which would you choose?

[ ] "We don't need robotics to achieve the efficiencies you need. I'll get you set up with my team and they'll lead your team through our design and build process."

[ ] "My team can qualify vendors and facilitate the discussions, but we're going to need updated requirements from your team. We've created a new process in the past year, and I want to make sure the documentation fits into our standard approach."

[ ] "This looks like a great opportunity to collaborate. I know when we've connected with your team in the past, they haven't been thrilled at the idea of new optimization projects. If a couple of members of my team and I could tour the facility and document some of the process from our vantage point, we'll be better equipped to qualify vendors and coordinate the robotics discussions, and we might catch some other opportunities to drive cost out of the process."

The first message dismisses Philippe's perspective and asserts that Mia's team is going to take over. The second puts the onus on Philippe's team to produce work before they receive partnership from Mia's team, placing a higher value on documentation than on partnership. The third demonstrates empathy and understanding of the context of Philippe's team, acknowledges and answers Philippe's request, and suggests beginning with partnership and joint proximity to increase shared understanding. None of the three are overloaded with technical jargon or attempts from Mia to credential herself or her team.

It is relatively easy to imagine the exponential number of breaking points within and across organizations when reading through these examples. It would have been natural and tempting for each leader to assert authority, credential themselves, or focus on their individual goals. By focusing on common goals that benefit the organization more broadly and leveraging shared language, leaders can avert many of the pitfalls that create inefficiencies and organizational divides that increase over time.

Three Altitudes of Inputs and Outputs

All technology, industry, and business processes can be broken down into inputs and outputs, and therefore a shared language across organizations.

Artificial intelligence, for example, is a broad field, with disciplines ranging from reinforcement learning to neural networks to clustering and new approaches, applications, and breakthroughs on a weekly, if not daily, basis. Many data scientists have made considerable effort and taken large portions of meetings to explain the finer points of an algorithm to their colleagues. There are times when these details are pertinent to the technologist's business and/or industry peers, but more often than not, breaking it down to inputs and outputs to support the decision that needs to be made would save time and better serve the goals of the organization.

In the case of a machine learning algorithm, the input could be location data and the output could be a clothing recommendation given the current weather. The underlying technology could be anything from a statistical model to decision trees, or a random forest classifier (to name a few).

In the case of a business process, the input could be an organizational change that needs to be made and the output could be a plan with guidance for leaders, managers, and individual contributors along with required training and updated incentives. The underlying process could be months or years of research and planning, analyzing the behavior of team members, performing surveys of the organization and analyzing the results from psychological, neurological, and organizational science perspectives.

In the case of an industry-specific process, the input could be sunlight shining on solar panels and the output could be electricity when a bedroom light is switched on. The underlying industry specifics include the conversion of energy, electrical wiring and casing, electrical currents, grounding, batteries, and much more.

The ability to break information down to its inputs and outputs is a key component of orchestrating experts across disciplines to achieve remarkable results. Figure 14.2 presents a structural framework for inputs and outputs that flows from the top altitude to the most granular. Organizations can benefit from starting with the top-level input and output as a baseline for communication across domains. Colleagues can then drill down to the depth that is needed to inform the decision being made or provide necessary awareness.

Over time, organizations will find their specific level of depth required to be understood across all three pillars for a decision to be made, although the average is likely less deep than an expert from a given field would assume.

Some of you might have one or more colleagues who immediately come to mind as experts who struggle to calibrate their communication to the accessible with guidance altitude, much less the universal. These colleagues

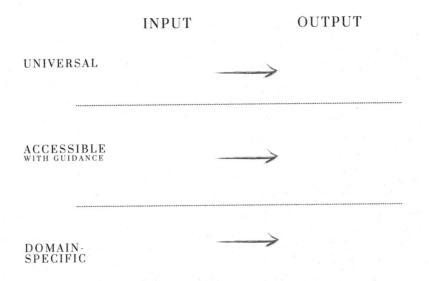

INPUT   OUTPUT

UNIVERSAL

ACCESSIBLE
WITH GUIDANCE

DOMAIN-
SPECIFIC

Figure 14.2   Three Altitudes of Inputs and Outputs

have mastered their craft, often steeped in research, application, and years of experience. Along the way, they can lose a sense of how little context others outside their field understand or need to understand in order to collaborate. More often than not, collaborations with these experts begin with the well-meaning intention to ensure that colleagues have enough context, and are unsure as to whether their colleagues will be able to ask the right questions and delve into the deeper layers of a topic as needed.

Each of us is a subject matter expert in our own field(s), and the imperative is on the individual to calibrate our discussions to the most effective altitude for the purpose of a given discussion.

Below are two examples. Where would you plot the altitude of these discussions and how effective do you feel these meetings would be?

Example A

The regional director of an organization's real estate/facilities management team is meeting with a data scientist and a facilities manager. The regional director has asked the team to find ways to reduce emissions across the organizational campus footprint.

The facilities manager opens the discussion with a review of the ask, then an overview of heating, ventilation, and air conditioning systems. He shares the science behind chillers and boilers, condensers, cooling towers, water flow rates, and wet bulb temperature readings. He feels it is important for the rest of the team to understand the factors, criteria, constraints, and control variables.

The data scientist then gives an overview of her process and approach. She starts with a beginner's guide to understanding statistical methods, what good data looks like, and considerations that would inform the length of time it would take to complete a project.

Example B

A senior manager and her team at a utilities company is meeting with a team from the internal information technology organization. She opens the meeting with the goal: they are hoping to use technology to modernize their approach to asset management. She shares that their current approach to replacing parts across the electric grid is static, based on manuals written 30 years ago. She and her team are hoping that there might be a way to predict when parts will fail and send technicians to fix and/or replace them. They believe this will lead to getting more use out of parts that wear and tear more slowly, and fewer outages by replacing parts with increased wear and tear prior to failure. Multiple billions of dollars are spent maintaining assets across the grid, and reducing this by even a single percentage point would make a material impact.

The data science team subsequently asks clarifying questions and begins sharing the kinds of machine learning algorithms that could be used to solve this problem. They share that a first-principles simulation of the grid could be created that would then serve as a testing ground for deep reinforcement learning to test various hypotheses in a simulated environment. They explain how deep learning and reinforcement learning have been put together to create a newer, more targeted discipline, and that the resulting neural network would likely be well-suited to this problem.

In Example A, the goal of the discussion, as set by the regional director, was put forth in universal terms. The facilities manager, however, dove much deeper into the specifics of his field than served the purpose of the meeting. The data scientist started in the domain-specific expertise with the overview of statistical methods, but then transitioned into accessible and ultimately universal. This is plotted in Figure 14.3.

In Example B, the senior manager gave enough context to make the subject matter accessible and relatable, as well as to assist her information technology peers in narrowing the scope of their questions and the partnership. The data science team starts and ends the discussion within the context of domain-specific language.

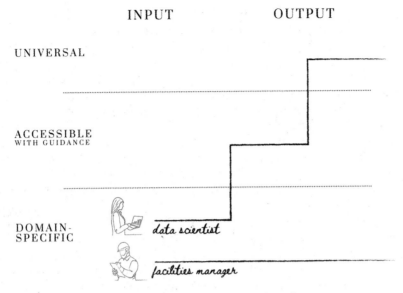

INPUT   OUTPUT

UNIVERSAL

ACCESSIBLE
WITH GUIDANCE

DOMAIN-
SPECIFIC   data scientist

                                facilities manager

Figure 14.3   Three Altitudes of Inputs and Outputs (Plotted)

In either example, the onus lies with the individual to correctly calibrate the altitude of their contributions to meet the varying levels of expertise within the room. In a meeting that consists solely of technical experts, for example, there is no need to venture out of domain-specific language. It is up to each individual to be aware of the altitude needed for a given meeting.

Managers and leaders have a different responsibility. Many have achieved their leadership purview based on their ability to understand cross-disciplinary language, confer with various experts, and make informed decisions. The limitation of this approach is that the leader's ability and bandwidth to understand, push for deeper insights, and ideate becomes the bottleneck through which innovation must funnel, especially given the time constraints faced by most leaders.

Facilitating and developing common language between these groups of experts will empower the organization with exponentially more valuable ideas and solutions, and is the leader's imperative in the era of Autonomous Transformation.

This is achieved by calibrating the altitude of the discussion, then simplifying through breaking the discussion down to inputs and outputs. The following is an example of this in action.

The information technology and manufacturing operations organizations at a manufacturer are meeting to determine how a new autonomous artificial intelligence capability might be leveraged for increased yield and reduced waste on the manufacturing line. A data scientist begins sharing specifics of the technology that the manufacturing operations leader feels is deeper than the team needs to understand. She interrupts the data scientist and remarks on his obvious expertise on the subject and asks if he can break it into simpler terms to make sure everyone can understand. The data scientist agrees, and the manufacturing operations leader proceeds to the whiteboard, draws the inputs and outputs framework, and shares an example from a manufacturing perspective: at the universal level, suppliers ship them raw steel (input), and they manufacture vehicle parts (output). At the accessible level and zoomed in on one of the areas where they have the most waste as an organization, the presence of variability in the process means that the machinery tends to get out of alignment at various points across the line (input). Because quality inspections are scheduled, sometimes they do not catch the problem until many flawed components have been manufactured that then need to be scrapped (output). She hands the whiteboard marker to the data scientist and asks if she can share what kind of technical inputs might be required to explore addressing this challenge, and what kind of outputs could be achieved.

If you decide to try this approach at your workplace, it will be important to avoid weaponizing the framework. Approaching the topic with vulnerability and consideration will be critical to building and maintaining trust with your peers or team members.

This work is nontrivial, and market leaders will be determined by the degree to which their leaders and managers master the ability to facilitate and develop common language between groups of experts to empower the organization with exponentially more valuable ideas and solutions.

Notes

1. J. P. Das, *Verbal Conditioning and Behaviour* (Oxford, UK: Pergamon Press, 2014), 92.
2. This example and others will be within the frame of problem solving to serve the function of conveying the idea in a familiar context.

PART SIX

Design for Inevitability

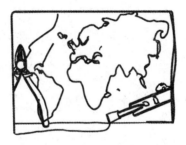

fire was not discovered
it was designed.

—HAROLD NELSON, IN *THE DESIGN WAY*

CHAPTER 15

From Data-Driven to Reason-Driven

> The precepts of management taught in business and engineering schools are that the only good decision is a data-based decision.
>
> —ROGER MARTIN

*D*ata-driven is an adjective that means "determined by or dependent on the collection or analysis of data."

The earliest documented collection of data in the workplace began in the late nineteenth century, when Frederick Taylor and his team of experts used stopwatches to collect information about the time it took laborers to achieve tasks—the first application of the scientific method in the context of business.

With the integration of machines in the workplace, the rise of computing power, and significant increases in methods of collecting, storing, and processing data, the term *data-driven* has become a mantra in leadership publications, management theory, and within and across organizations.

Data-driven decisions can begin with observed patterns in data trending in an undesired direction, or they can begin with a hypothesis, a need, or a question, but they always end with a set of numbers that justify a decision.

In other words, data-driven is an inherently mechanistic paradigm.

While consulting a large telecommunications company, I observed a data-driven decision that began with a need. The customer service organization needed to reduce costs.

What ensued was a data-driven process, breaking down and analyzing the costs of the customer service department. It was determined that the most basic and important unit of variable cost in the department was increments of time an agent spent on the phone with a customer.

The next step was analyzing all the reasons customers called in and therefore required time spent on the phone with an agent. Once the categorized data came back, the data was first ranked by the number of calls, then by the average amount of time taken to resolve calls within each category. One of the most expensive categories was callers dialing in to make a late payment over the phone.

It was hypothesized that if the automated system that first answered the phone call checked the incoming number against an internal database and, if the customer was late on their payment, provided an automated option to make a late payment, it could reduce costs on the order of tens of millions of dollars.

The solution was implemented and the hypothesis was proven correct. The organization saved tens of millions of dollars a year from implementing a few lines of code.

Examples like this tend to excite managers and leaders, who turn to their team members and direct that all decisions henceforth will only be data-driven decisions.

Aristotle's Conundrum

Aristotle was the first scientist. His invention of the scientific method has become the basis not only for the field of science, but also for organizational decision-making.

If a decision-maker is asked to invest in a given initiative, the ensuing questions will gather data about the proposed initiative, including measures such as the projected length of time, financial investment, and return on investment. The degree to which a data-driven answer can be provided to these questions is commensurate with the amount of historical data exists or is available.

If a company wanted to launch a new marketing website, for example, the skill set required, the cost of hosting the website on a server, the projected costs if there is a surge in traffic to the website, the development time—each of these can be calculated because of the decades of previous web development initiatives and the ubiquity of web development skills and expertise.

In the arena of emerging technologies, autonomous or otherwise, the more groundbreaking and differentiating a technological application, the less there will be historical data against which to make predictions and therefore base decisions.

Within the context of maintenance mode or a reformational initiative, data-driven analysis is well-suited for identifying opportunities for incremental improvement of an existing system.

Where data-driven analysis becomes not only less effective but counterproductive is in its rigorous application across all initiatives as a gate-keeping mechanism, leading to a form of organizational empiricism.

Returning to the context of science, scientists cannot prove a hypothesis and a projected return on investment before they have received funding to execute the scientific method of defining the question, gathering information, forming hypotheses, conducting experiments to test hypotheses, analyzing the data, interpreting data, and publishing their results.

Translating that context into initiatives that involve the application of advanced technologies, such as artificial intelligence, technology initiatives tend to fall into four categories. The first category is when a given technology is unknown or new to the organization and is therefore treated as an experiment with little to no investment, visualized in Figure 15.1 as the "Technology Proving Ground (PoCs [Proofs of Concept])." The second category is high-value initiatives with low levels of complexity, meaning it has been become a well-established application of the technology in the industry, such as web development. These kinds of investments fit neatly into return-on-investment calculations and organizational leaders are encouraged and incented to pursue them. The third category is high-value initiatives that are highly complex. These initiatives are discouraged and disincentivized in most organizations for fear that they ultimately end up in the "Career Threatening" square of the quadrant, yielding low value after considerable investment.

In Figure 15.2, additional distinctions are added to the top two squares in the quadrant. In order to have high confidence that a technology initiative will add high value in a low amount of time, or, put another way, the only way to have a data-driven justification for investment in a new technological

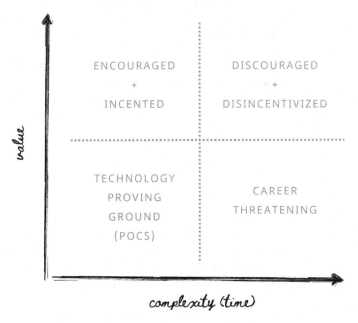

Figure 15.1   Data-Driven Justification Matrix

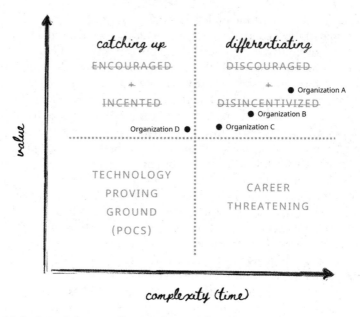

Figure 15.2   Data-Driven Justification Matrix (Plotted)

application is if other organizations have already invested in and realized value from it, the differentiation of which decreases with each subsequent implementation in parallel with a decrease in complexity and uncertainty until it moves into the "Catching Up" square of the quadrant. Few leaders who manage their organizations in this manner would replace their organization's tagline with "Chasing the wake of others," but this is the reality of this approach, as the data on which to base data-driven decisions is only formed in the wake of another organization leading the way into the unknown and generating that data.

Organizational Empiricism

Empiricism is a philosophical theory that all knowledge originates in experience. Organizations around the world, in the process of embedding data-driven principles into every aspect of decision-making, have developed a form of organizational empiricism, in which the only way a new product, service line, or initiative can be funded is if the future value can be empirically proven.

This is a logical fallacy, as you cannot have empirical proof of something that has yet to occur, and it is self-preserving in the case that the initiative is not successful. Leaders can justify that they approved the initiative based on the empirically sound proposal, and the logical end is that the blame lay on the person or team who formed the proposal, either through failure to adequately gather and analyze the necessary data or failure in execution.

Leaders who only understand and are able to reward data-driven decisions will curate their organizations to optimize their existing core value propositions. Data-driven decision-making is a foundational capability for any effective leader or manager, but it only allows for tuning and fixing that which already exists. In order for leaders and organizations to innovate and create, especially in the context of the unknowable, such as with new technologies, data-driven decision-making must be extended and augmented with reason.

Organizational Reasoning (from Data-Driven to Reason-Driven)

The antidote to the inherently mechanistic nature of being data-driven can be found in the human discipline of reasoning. Reasoning is the drawing of inferences or conclusions through the use of reason, which is defined as the power of comprehending, inferring, or thinking, especially in orderly rational ways.[1,2]

Replacing organizational empiricism with organizational reasoning adds humans back into the equation of decision-making. In the empirical paradigm, the person or team forming the proposal only serves in a data-gathering and computational capacity. The decision is then based on the mathematics, and not the opinions or reasoning of the people who researched the options or created the proposal. In practice, many leaders will pause after reviewing the numbers and ask their team members what they think. If they agree with the team's logic, but do not feel that the logic is substantiated by data in the proposal, they may ask their teams to update the proposal in specific ways they feel they will be able to justify to their leadership, but the process itself does not support decisions that must be justified based on something other than data.

Organizational reasoning is a step in unwinding and replacing the mechanistic worldview with a social systems worldview, as it places human reasoning at the top of the hierarchy of decision-making, on the foundation of data-driven methodologies where appropriate. This begins with the knowledge that empiricism in the context of a new initiative is a logical fallacy, and pivots to rely on the logic and reasoning of an organization's experts, supported by data where available. This can be represented rigorously in a proposal, and there have already been steps in this direction, such as documented assumptions.

An example of the applicability of this approach would be in the context of a leadership directive to eliminate carbon emissions across the organization by 2030. Since the organization has not already eliminated carbon emissions, proposed solutions cannot be empirically proven. Furthermore, neither the cost of elimination of carbon emissions nor its ensuing impact to customer acquisition and retention can be accurately predicted.

A proposal in accordance with the process of organizational reasoning would begin with an examination of that which is known and can be represented based on empirical data, such as the current carbon emissions, broken down by scopes one, two, and three, and across categories such as lines of business, geographies, facilities, and travel. Other areas that can be represented empirically in this context are the benchmarking of the organization's emissions against other organizations within the industry vertical, the top methods being applied to reduce emissions within the industry with readouts of the results where available, governmental grant programs to assist with reducing carbon emissions, the state of science and research on developing further methods, and the current guidance and recommendations from research institutes, governmental agencies, advisors, partners, and academic leaders.

From the edges of what is known in the above, the person or team developing this plan can begin conducting reasoning experiments, working backwards from the future point in which the organization has no carbon emissions by the year 2030 to determine a set of theories that would need to be true to reach this future, and the successive theories and hypotheses that would also need to be true. Through this process, an organizational reasoning tree begins to take shape, based on logical inferences against which hypotheses can be shared, developed, and further explored to determine the degrees of confidence of different paths. This creates a foundation on which creative discussion can be bridged with rigor and documentation, and pivots the conversation from solely discussing the validity of conclusions to a higher order of human thought and experience, in the discussion of hypotheses. Forming strategies through this approach brings others into the entire thread of reasoning, which is much more difficult to do verbally than visually, and can be shared with stakeholders and team members to generate consensus, which will improve the likelihood of positive collaboration and follow-through.

This is arguably a more scientific process than the established processes for data-driven decision-making as it includes the process of asking questions and generating theories.

The organizational reasoning tree, as demonstrated in Figure 15.3, developed through this process could then be updated as the organization engaged in initiatives to test and validate hypotheses, and new theories, hypotheses and branches of successive logical inferences could be added continuously (see Figure 15.4). This presents a foundation for a new bridge between the centuries of reasoning theory and methodological development and the practical environment of organizations, creating a dynamic representation of the organization's strategy, assumptions, knowns, and unknowns as the organization progresses boldly into a future driven by reason.

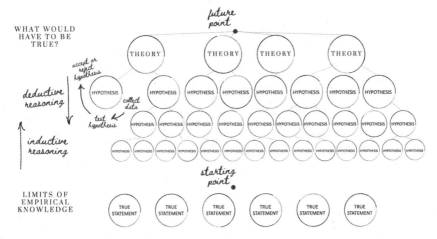

Figure 15.3   Organizational Reasoning Tree

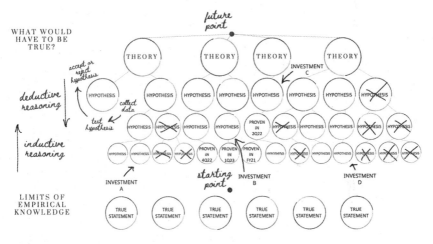

Figure 15.4   Organizational Reasoning Tree (Plotted)

Notes

1. "Reasoning," Merriam-Webster Dictionary, https://www.merriam-webster.com/dictionary/reasoning (accessed January 10, 2023).
2. "Reason," Merriam-Webster Dictionary, https://www.merriam-webster.com/dictionary/reason (accessed January 10, 2023).

CHAPTER 16

The Reformational Economics of Linear and Exponential Value

As organizations transition from being data-driven to reason-driven in the era of Autonomous Transformation, one of the most entrenched paradigms that will need to shift is individual organizational linear return on investment calculations and required justification in order to receive funding.

This economic paradigm follows the logical, data-driven concept that organizations should only invest in initiatives that can rigorously demonstrate the path to return on investment with a certain timeline. One of the organizations I have been a part of required the demonstration of 10 times the investment within three years, or the initiative would not be funded.

This kind of requirement naturally leads an organization down the path toward maintenance mode, and when experts and leaders conceive of acts of creation or transformation that will not be able to justify investment within this paradigm, but that they feel are important to the evolution of the market or their own careers, this construct naturally propels these kinds of groups out of the organization to build the idea from scratch and without oversight.

This focus on achieving short-term, measurable results narrows the aperture to incremental improvements, to the exclusion of strategic investments that may not yield immediate benefits. This has systemic roots, as it is based on and reinforced by individual and organizational economic incentives for which leaders and managers are held accountable in quarterly and annual performance reviews. However, this short-sighted approach can have negative long-term effects, especially regarding latent economic potential, as demonstrated in Figure 16.1.

This illustration demonstrates that profit follows a similar natural arc as gravity. Focusing on achieving the highest possible profit in the short term threatens long-term profitability and limits economic potential.

It took Amazon, ranked the fifth most valuable public company in the world at the time of this writing, nine and a half years before it reported its first profitable quarter.[1]

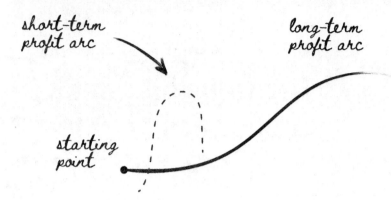

Figure 16.1   Profit Arc

Most are used to the idea of a startup working toward profitability, but there are examples of organizations making long-term investments, such as Microsoft's search engine, Bing, which was launched in 2009, reported its first profit in 2015, and in 2023, has become a central component to Microsoft's long-term artificial intelligence strategic partnership with OpenAI.

If we were to create a list of products and services in our daily lives that would not exist if someone had not decided to sacrifice short-term profit, it would fill up many pages. A review of the past such as this is often met with hindsight bias, defined as "the tendency, upon learning an outcome of an event, to overestimate one's ability to have foreseen the outcome."[2] An alternative exercise would be to imagine a list of the products and services that might exist if someone had decided to sacrifice short-term profit.

These kinds of strategic bets are being made, but against the system, and at great personal risk for those who have argued for and made them. If the system could be transformed to provide an accounting framework that, in practice and not just theory, differentiated between investments in short-term and long-term value, measuring for the latter in directional milestones and reason, which requires trust in human reasoning and not only computation, organizations can take a strategic step toward disentangling from the mechanistic worldview of the Industrial Revolution, engineering social systemic dynamics to support a more human future, which would fundamentally transform the way organizations create and sustain value in the market.

Linear versus Exponential Value in the Case of Capability

The paradigm of short-term, linear return on investment calculations, in the context of technology, plays a significant role in inhibiting long-term value for two primary reasons.

First, technological capabilities are interdependent. Investments in the context of technology, as illustrated in Figure 16.2, lay the groundwork for future initiatives that would not be possible without the initial investment, but that are not traditionally included in the return-on-investment calculation.

Second, technological capabilities span functions and suborganizations, but justifications are traditionally based on individual use cases within a specific organization. If Organizations A and B could both benefit from investments in building data science capabilities, for example, and in the absence of preexisting data science capabilities within the organization, the investment justification for Organizations A and B, each taken separately, might both be rejected. Taken together, however, the development of the capability for one organization could significantly reduce the cost for the second organization, rendering a net positive impact to the overall organization.

In the context of justifying the development of technological capability, new economic models need to be developed that account for the long-term, systemic impact of the proposed capability across the entire organization, as opposed to only accounting for the localized, short-term impact to a part of the system.

In the context of Autonomous Transformation, leaders who have gone through the process of solving for the future of their industry and how their organization can best serve its core function within that future will then need to set a strategy, through a process such as organizational reasoning, to leverage acts of creation and the processes of reformation and transformation to realize that vision.

When this strategy has been set, if it is sieved through the rest of the organization, unchanged from the average worldview and processes of organizations in today's context, what emerges out the other side of that process may be unrecognizable.

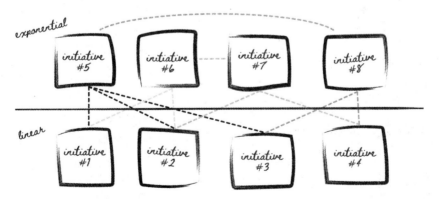

Figure 16.2   Linear vs. Exponential Value

Figure 16.3 Linear Value Staircase

Figure 16.3 was created to facilitate conversation, together with Figures 16.1 and 16.2, to shift this economic paradigm over time. Once a desired future has been determined, and a strategy has been developed, if the organizational process then proceeds to use an analytic process to break down each individual initiative required to reach that future, aggregating the return on investment of each individual initiative to attempt to model and understand the return on the whole transformation, this figure can serve to illustrate the need to "buy the whole staircase."

When architecting a home or a skyscraper, architects are not expected to model out and justify the expense of each individual step that makes up a staircase. For each level of the home, there needs to be a way to travel from one level to another.

If an organization has determined that they want to climb to a higher tier of value creation, the same holds true for them. This does not mean that they cannot make strategic and tactical choices in how they design and build "the staircase," but the conversational pivot from the analysis-based "step" to the synthesis-based "staircase" may be required to justify and account for investing in and reaching the long-term, transformational goal of the organization.

Notes

1. J. C. Perez, "Amazon Records First Profitable Year in Its History," *ComputerWorld*, January 28, 2004, https://www.computerworld.com/article/2575106/amazon-records-first-profitable-year-in-its-history.html (accessed February 10, 2023).
2. Mary Inman, "Hindsight Bias," *Encyclopedia Britannica*, February 3, 2023, https://www.britannica.com/topic/hindsight-bias (accessed February 10, 2023).

CHAPTER 17

The Reformational Economics of Omission and Commission

> For executives who want to maximize their job security in a public or private organization that deprecates mistakes and ignores errors of omission, the best strategy is to do nothing or as little as possible.
> —Dr. Russell Ackoff, in *Transforming the Systems Movement*

Most people are familiar with the fact that Blockbuster passed on opportunities to acquire Netflix in 2000. What most people do not know is that Blockbuster built a streaming service 12 years before Netflix did that never made it to market.

When Ron Norris, a consulting executive whose team had designed, built, and successfully piloted the first streaming service in 1995 on behalf of Blockbuster (called Blockbuster on Demand), received a call from a senior executive with oversight of the program, he expected a congratulations, gratitude, and questions about how quickly he and his team could bring this to market.

Instead, he was directed to cancel the initiative altogether.

The executive informed him that the new offering would eliminate late fees, which accounted for 12% of Blockbuster's revenue and was therefore not a suitable path forward.

When Blockbuster filed for bankruptcy in 2010, this executive may have remembered the conversation he had with Norris and imagined how differently things would have turned out had he not chosen to cancel the initiative, but one thing is certain: that decision, despite disastrous consequences to the organization, had no negative impact, aside from opportunity cost, on the finances or reputation of the executive responsible.

This is because leaders and organizations are measured on their errors of commission, actions they took, but not their errors of omission, actions they did not take.

It is even likely that this executive included a bullet point about protecting 12% of annual revenue in his annual review.

Errors of omission have a higher impact than errors of commission. They are a shadow force with the power to end an organization. As organizational leaders make decisions, they are not aware of what they are not seeing—the risks they are not taking and learning from. Their errors of commission and their successes become a self-affirming loop until an internal leader disrupts the pattern, or the accumulated errors of omission have grown large enough to pave the path for a new organization to rise and overtake the legacy organization in the market.

I mentioned in Chapter 16 that in the context of Autonomous Transformation, leaders who set a vision for the future of the organization and a strategy to realize that future face the risk that, as their strategy runs its course through the organization's process of translating strategy into action, the current worldview and processes may produce an unrecognizable translation that is not fit for the purpose of creating the leader's desired future.

One of the paradigms that comprises these processes is that accounting systems only record acts of commission.

What did it cost Blockbuster to acquire Erol's in 1990?

What did it cost Blockbuster not to move forward with Blockbuster on Demand in 1995?

What did it cost Blockbuster not to acquire Netflix in 2000?

The first question can be answered in moments with an Internet search. The second and third? They can be modeled in hindsight, but were not accounted for at the time.

In the era of artificial intelligence and the steep rise in complexity across many advanced technologies, accounting only for the risks taken nudges leaders toward maintenance mode. Some leaders ignore this nudge, at great personal risk, because they have a vision they consider to be worth spending their social capital on to step outside of the organization's formal accounting process to bring their vision to fruition.

A social systemic alternative to this approach would be to account for every act of omission alongside every act of commission. As those on either side of the hierarchy of a given decision-maker present decisions to be made, those decisions, including the other options that were presented, can be recorded.

On a regular cadence, the decision-maker and team can review the impact of the acts of commission together with the considered impacts of the acts of omission, which can be researched in advance of the meeting. This could create a forum in which the team can discuss and learn, and the decision-making capabilities of the whole social system can improve.

Imagine if, in considering which leader should be promoted to the executive leadership team, the deciding committee could look to the organization's accounting system for a report on the net impact that leader has had on the organization, not only with the funded initiatives and whether or not they were successful, but with the initiatives that were not funded and the acquisitions or partnerships that did not move forward. This would create a more holistic picture of the individual's ability to discern strategic and tactical investments on behalf of the organization.

From a systemic perspective, this kind of accounting approach would systemically nudge decision-makers toward organizational reasoning to create, socialize, and document the application of reason in the decision-making process in order to keep a record of *why* a decision was made to accompany the record of *what* decision was made.

Outcome Bias in the Face of Failure

Another organizational dynamic that naturally arises from the emphasis on acts of commission and the disregard of acts of omission is the application of outcome bias when initiatives do not go well.

Outcome bias places less importance on the events preceding outcomes and elevates the importance of the outcome itself when examining a past decision.

This contributes to an organizational culture that unfairly punishes leaders and teams whose initiatives do not go as planned based solely on the outcome, and not on the quality of the plan or on the quality of the execution.

Examining failure through a lens that includes the broader context, such as the quality of design and execution, there are four types of failure:

1. Well designed but poorly executed
2. Poorly designed but well executed
3. Poorly designed and poorly executed
4. Well designed and well executed

Leaders and managers who overcome outcome bias and examine the results of a failed initiative through this lens can provide coaching targeted at the preceding events and broader context of the failure to improve the team's ability to design and execute initiatives in the future (see Figure 17.1).

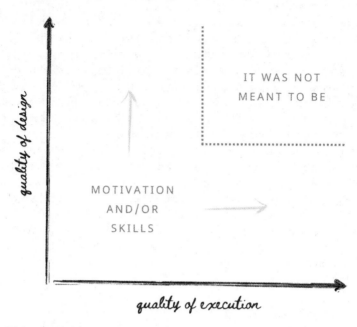

Figure 17.1   An Antidote to Outcome Bias

Conversely, punishing failure for any reason other than what is shown in the bottom-left quadrant of the figure turns off the innovative part of an organization. If an initiative was well-designed and well-executed, but still failed, the reason likely has more to do with the broader systemic context than the team, the understanding of which, through the application of synthesis and analysis together with the team, could yield valuable insights on broader systemic dynamics that need to be reformed, transformed, or created.

CHAPTER 18

The Ecosystem: Surprising and Remarkable Partnerships

There are specializations, there are skills, and not everything can be contained within one company. You have to rely on the ecosystem. And the ecosystem is a test. If you cannot get the ecosystem going, it will tell you where things are going to fail for you. A viable ecosystem is one where all the different entities have an economically viable model at different levels of profitability.

—GURDEEP PALL

Imagine if Michael Jordan showed up to a one-on-one basketball tournament in 1990, laced up his shoes, played a pump-up song in the locker room, and raced out onto the court, fired up, only to realize that this was a five-on-five tournament, and not a one-on-one tournament.

This happens in the market on a regular, if not daily, basis.

Organizations form surprising and remarkable alliances, leveraging their combined core competencies, channels, investments, and brands to form an ecosystem, pivoting the competitive dynamic from organizations competing against each other head-to-head to an organization competing against an entire ecosystem of organizations.

The intentional design and development of an ecosystem serves not only a competitive function, but also in building market dynamics that contribute to the inevitability of a future that requires more than one organization to bring to pass.

Designing for Inevitability: An Ecosystemic Discipline

When a person or organization envisions a future they would like to bring to fruition, such as in the combined processes of future solving, functional reimagining, and organizational reasoning, in asking and answering the question "What would have to be true to achieve this future?" and in determining subsequent theories and hypotheses against which to reason and test, if that future has any range of depth and breadth, there will be dynamics outside the control of that person and organization that can either be accounted for within the construct of a collaborative ecosystem, or unaccounted for and only monitored in hopes that the progression of these dynamics will support the envisioned future.

These dynamics, unchecked, assuming no market disruptions or upheavals, will follow the direction and vision of the organizations that have the most influence and strongest vision over the segment of the market in which that dynamic is at play. If partnerships are formed that account for a subset of market dynamics that most contribute to the likelihood of creating an envisioned future, organizational reasoning can evolve to ecosystem reasoning, in which a broader future, that of the ecosystem, is envisioned, the function of that ecosystem reimagined in the broader context such as the market and society, leading to the development of theories and hypotheses to be tested and proved and disproved in a context of joint investment and accountability.

Building an Ecosystem

The first step in building an ecosystem should begin without the context of an existing ecosystem, instead focusing on what ecosystem would best support the envisioned future of the organization.

If an organization has solved for the future it would like to bring to fruition, reimagining or reforming its function within the context of the systems in which it exists, such as the economic system, the market, and the education system, and the organization has created an organizational reasoning tree or trees, the developed strategy will hint, both directly and indirectly, as to what would be required of an ecosystem and therefore what functions the other players within the ecosystem would need to serve.

There is a variant form of chess referred to as "Bughouse," which is played on two chessboards by four chess players broken into teams of two. This form of chess is so popular that most tournaments include a Bughouse tournament (along with a speed chess tournament) in the days preceding the main event. Bughouse retains all of the rules of traditional chess, with the addition of a few extras. The core additions start with the ability to pass any captured pieces to one's partner, who is playing as the opposite color. In the next move or any time after, each player can either make a normal move with the pieces on the board or place a piece captured by their partner on the board instead of moving one of the existing pieces. Once any player is checkmated, the opposing team wins the match. This means that if I see that my partner could checkmate her opponent if only she had a pawn, I could take a pawn regardless of how well it was protected, sacrificing a higher-value piece in order to hand my partner the pawn, which could then be placed on the board to win the game.

In building an ecosystem, this analogy represents an organization that begins with any subset of pieces on the board of the market or whichever broader system(s) of which it is a part. After having envisioned and set its sights on a desired future, the organization can subsequently assess what pieces would be required to make the envisioned future inevitable (or as close to inevitable as possible). This can then be examined against the existing pieces on the board to determine whether those pieces are sufficient, or if other functioning parts of the ecosystem need to be partnered with or created.

The next step necessitates an understanding that an organizational ecosystem is a social system, and each organization is also a social system, made up of individual people with a vast array of worldviews, values, skills, priorities, and modes of working.

Building an ecosystem is an act of orchestrating those social dynamics, fueled by values and on the foundation of economic viability in order to achieve a shared vision for the future.

Maintaining versus Sustaining an Ecosystem

One of the pitfalls to be wary of when working in a position aligned to the development and management of an ecosystem lies in interacting with ecosystem partners mechanistically instead of socially, or as machines within a broader machine (maintaining) instead of as humans within a social system (sustaining).

This takes place when managers and leaders responsible for the partnership between two organizations focus on actions instead of interactions. If a technology organization, for example, partners with and certifies a consulting firm to deliver solutions with their technology, one aspect of the partnership will likely include setting the strategy for and executing joint business development. In building internal dashboards across partners, a data-driven approach would list the partners, ranked by the number of sourced and closed sales deals.

This metric is not unimportant, but if discussions and business reviews with partners are focused on the number of sourced and closed deals, the number of certified solution architects, and even the number of projects that have made it into production, this is reductionist thinking, which assumes that cause-and-effect relationships are simple and predictable: if we can get more deals in the pipeline and more solution architects trained, we will close more deals. And if we close more deals, we will get more projects into production.

Systems thinking takes the more complex dynamics into account, focusing instead on the interactions between the parts and the performance of the system as a whole. If a partner is pushed to get more deals in the pipeline, the pressure could result in fewer qualified deals, producing the same or fewer closed deals; and if they are required to produce more solution architects by a certain date for a product they are still uncertain is going to turn into a viable practice for them, they may put junior solution architects through the training to meet the number and rely on architects from the technology organization to deliver and train their architects until they see a stronger and proven economic opportunity that justifies pivoting their strongest-performing solution architects from consistent, billable work to a new, unproven product and partnership.

What would have to be true for the parts to better interact to achieve the desired outcome?

A social systems vantage point starts with asking a question unrelated to the number of sourced deals or any number, but about the humans that comprise the partner organization and how they make decisions, for example. What would have to be true to warrant a greater investment from this partner? What vision or signal would they need to see in order to bring this product to their top customers for whom they are a trusted advisor?

These are social questions, and the answers will vary significantly based on partners even within a specific technology or industry vertical. This is more complex than managing all organizations in the same manner based on a set of metrics and threatening to end partnerships with partners who do not meet certain metrics within a specified timeline, but yields significant long-term impact on individual and organizational ability to form and sustain partnerships that achieve meaningful impact.

This lens can be combined with the idea of seeing all the pieces on a chessboard, as treating every partner in the same manner and requiring them to follow the same process detracts from or eliminates the ability or interest for that organization to leverage their full set of pieces.

I observed this firsthand when a large organization was interested in partnering with a technology product team. They were discussing acquiring one of the smaller partners who had been partnered with the technology product team for years and had become a key partner, but when their request to meet with leadership and set a shared vision at the onset of the partnership was met with the instruction that they would need to go through the same process as the other partners who were a fraction of a percent of their size, they lost interest in bringing their whole chess set to bear for that partnership. The technology organization's desire for uniformity took precedence over engagement with their partners as fellow social systems with whom they could develop and sustain a symbiotic ecosystem.

Surprising and Remarkable Partnerships within an Organization

In the consumer market, Apple is an elegant example of systemic orchestration, so much so that this is baked into the very interactions of their products. If a user wants to pause a movie on an AppleTV device and they have misplaced the remote, they can pause or navigate the television with their Apple Watch or iPhone. The memorable aspect of this story is not the performance of any of these individual products, but their interaction. The degree to which systemic design has been applied across their product set is memorable, and no doubt has contributed to their sustained market leadership position. Apple changed the consumer electronics dynamic from a string of disconnected products to choosing between ecosystems. Instead of asking only "Which smartphone has the best performance?," customers are asking "Where will I watch my movies, play my games, store my images and videos, communicate with friends and family, track my fitness, and listen to my music?"

This kind of remarkable product ecosystem can only exist in the context of an organization that has developed a strong internal ecosystem, with surprising and remarkable partnerships. The idea that a watch should be able to navigate television controls is a surprising one, and remarkably useful when a customer comes across a situation in which that would be the easiest way to navigate the television.

The process of envisioning the future, determining which pieces would need to be on the board, and subsequently examining which pieces would need to be partnered with or created can be applied within organizations, yielding surprising and remarkable market dynamics for clients and customers with a higher degree of agility and joint focus than is possible in partnering with external organizations. Organizations can apply this approach within the safety of the internal organization to develop methodologies and to test and prove or disprove various models, frameworks, theories, and hypotheses, increasing the likelihood of successfully engaging with, building, and sustaining external ecosystems.

PART SEVEN
Create a More Human Future

The creation of the world did not take place once and for all time, but takes place every day.

—SAMUEL BECKETT, IN *PROUST*

CHAPTER 19

Beyond Pilot Purgatory

Purgatory is a state of existence in which a person or object remains suspended between two distinct states of being.

Pilots are often considered the proving ground for technologies. The logical premise is that a technology can be "piloted," the same way a television series is piloted, to test its applicability to the organization. Technology companies and consulting firms have invested heavily within this premise over the years to demonstrate the value of their solutions to potential customers.

A staggering number of these pilots, however, even when they meet the required benchmarks and advance beyond the pilot stage, never make it into production. While the specific data for this is difficult to track down (this is not a metric organizations tend to share publicly), it is commonly understood and referred to across industries, and is directionally represented by the statistic that only 13% of data science projects make it into production.[1]

Within the context of a mechanistic worldview, a pilot is a test of the viability of a technology or solution in the same way that a machine would be piloted to demonstrate its value.

But it is more than that.

Pilots within Social Systems

A technology or solution pilot is a social engagement between two or more parties, in which one party is endeavoring to earn the right to do business with another party. Unlike a machine test, which relies solely on the performance of the machine, a technology or solution pilot relies on the interaction between those demonstrating and those testing the viability of the technology.

A data science pilot, for example, begins with the process of designing the experiment, which involves a number of social interactions internal and external to the organization while choosing the use case, measuring the existing performance benchmark against which the solution will be tested, building the team, and proposing a shared timeline. This is a social engagement between organizations in which the social dynamic, regardless of individual intentions, is fraught with undue tension. Fundamentally, an external organization is asking or being asked to prove that they are able to outperform the existing work with the same data and/or systems, but without the internal network of relationships or domain expertise. Furthermore, depending on the organization and the construct of the pilot, friction internal to the organization can present itself, such as if a technology is being piloted without the knowledge of the information technology (IT) organization or if the technology goes against the prevailing technology strategy across the organization.

Once the experiment has been designed, its success relies on the ability of the technology or consulting organization's data science team to access the necessary data, and just as importantly, to understand the data, the broader context in which the data is generated, and what it represents. This requires interaction with domain experts, business leaders, and managers within the potential customer's organization.

This challenge is compounded in situations layered with additional social dynamics, such as Data Science Taylorism, where data scientists and experts do not believe they need to speak with domain experts, and that they only need access to the data to know all that they will need to know to complete the pilot and demonstrate value.

This behavior can also stem as a defensive mechanism to the pilot construct. If a given data science manager has faced undue criticism due not to their work, but to the natural direction of the social construct of a pilot, defensive maneuvers that eliminate social interaction within the prospective customer organization can begin to take shape. This harms the likelihood of pilot success and of production deployment in the long term.

Riskless Experimentation

If an organization does not need a new capability in order to get to a desired future, a pilot becomes an interesting-at-best, riskless experiment conducted in a controlled environment with limited scope and resources.

This strategy hedges the organizational leader approving the experiment by removing the risk if the pilot does not achieve its goals and, ironically, also almost guarantees that the pilot will not achieve its goals.

Technology projects require domain expertise in order to create value. Domain experts typically do not have extra bandwidth to dedicate the necessary time to share expertise with technologists building a pilot that is not guaranteed to be successful and ultimately make an impact on the broader organization. This can lead to a self-defeating cycle.

Efforts to lower risk also have a natural tendency to direct pilot initiatives toward use cases that are not essential to the present or the future of the organization, which places the pilot at the bottom of the list of organizational priorities. When pilots inevitably face the need for greater support upward or across the organization, leaders from across the company are naturally and logically incented to deprioritize dedicating their resources or social capital to support anything deemed "experimental."

Piloting the Path to Promotion

Some organizational leaders have seen pilots as a means of securing promotion within their organization. This involves leveraging investment from one or more technology and/or consulting firms to demonstrate the value of their platform or solution across a set of challenges the organization is facing. When one or more of the pilots meets its targeted metrics, the leader or manager can present the findings to their leaders and the broader organization with a planned path forward, and claim the vision not only of designing the pilot but also leveraging external investment.

This design pattern is common enough that many external consultants have fostered symbiotic relationships with up-and-coming leaders, to whom they are happy to give all credit as long as there is a steady flow of billable hours.

When this works, both the organizational leader and the supporting external organization are happy and feel proud of the result.

There are several issues with this approach, however:

1. The nature with which a pilot with this goal is set up means that the only path to escalation in order to overcome a challenge is disclosing the pilot and diffusing its element of surprise and awe, which incents organizational leaders to try ineffective methods of overcoming challenges.

2. When peers learn about a pilot that has been devised in this manner and with this goal, they, at best, offer resources or help despite the incentive not to, and at worst, are incented to intentionally derail the pilot.

3. Even if a pilot is successful in technical terms, when the organizational leaders attempt to raise broader awareness and secure investment to move the pilot forward, it can be shut down by leadership, either directly within or adjacent to the organization in which the pilot took place.

4. A pilot of this nature, by design, cannot get buy-in and collaboration from broader organizational stakeholders, which is a fundamental input to any successful organizational initiative.

5. The pilot could also aim in a direction that overlaps or contradicts other investments being made by the organization, and could therefore be shut down regardless of its ability to achieve its targeted objectives.

Human-Centered Transformation

Because organizations are social systems, the path to overcoming pilot purgatory begins with a decisive step away from the mechanistic concept of a pilot, which focuses on choosing a problem to solve or a use case, deciding what metrics can be measured to determine if the problem was adequately solved, paired with a data-driven analysis of a projected return on investment, a timeline, and so on.

An approach better suited to a social system—a human-centered approach—begins with the forming or reforming of the center of the social system around which the future of the organization can begin to transform through a combination of both designed and organic butterfly effects.

The Executive Committee for Human-Centered Transformation is that center. As demonstrated in Figure 19.1, the committee is designed to anchor on leadership voices from across the business, industry, and technology groups, led by a C-level executive sponsor, with the inclusion of external voices as best fits the ecosystem of a given organization and the future it wishes to design, represented in the figure as a managing partner of an advisory firm and an academic leader, which could be replaced by other voices. The same holds true for the rest of the diagram, which is intended as a directional guide to be translated into the specific context of an organization.

By creating a miniature model of the organization at the executive level with joint accountability for shared objectives, leaders can begin solving for the future of their industry and organization, and any broad-sweeping organizational changes that would be required in order to achieve that future can begin within this context, and be subsequently carried out throughout the organization until those changes accrue to a meaningful transformation across the overarching organization.

Transitioning from being a data-driven to a reason-driven organization (from Chapter 15), for example, would begin with a subset of organizational leaders such as this determining the future it wants to bring about for the broader organization, forming theories and hypotheses to be assigned across

Figure 19.1   Executive Committee for Human-Centered Transformation

organizations to then be supported by the creation, testing, and validation of additional hypotheses, and so on, until the culture of the organization transforms from being data-driven to reason-driven.

This construct can and should continue to transform and evolve as the nucleus around which the organization pivots in leading and reacting to market forces and dynamics, which will be reflected by the people and organizations represented within the executive committee.

This committee, while most effective when chaired by leaders with the broadest purview across the organization, can begin at any level within the organization to begin to drive meaningful change.

Note

1. VB Staff, "Why Do 87% of Data Science Projects Never Make It into Production?," *Venture Beat*, July 19, 2019, https://venturebeat.com/ai/why-do-87-of-data-science-projects-never-make-it-into-production (accessed October 17, 2022).

CHAPTER 20

Storytelling: Leading Social Systems

Storytelling enables different swaths of the population to all care about the same issue by meeting them where they are and drawing them in.

—Liz Fosslien

As organizations disentangle from the mechanistic worldview rooted in the Industrial Revolution in favor of a social systemic worldview, storytelling rises from extracurricular to a core means of leading social systems.

In this context, the effectiveness of leaders can be predicted as a function of the quality of their vision multiplied by their ability to translate that vision into a compelling story and draw others in.

Since the development of language, stories have been foundational to social systems, creating shared meaning, belonging, and purpose. They have also been among the most powerful agents of change throughout history, forming central themes and mantras around which people have connected and taken action.

Storytelling as a Strategic Organizational Imperative

In the context of an organization, story is foundational, with conscious and subconscious influences on individual and group behavior ranging from purchasing decisions to collaboration style in meetings, front-line behavior, and employee sense of purpose and belonging.

More than ever before, due to the ubiquity of the Internet, people are able to create and sustain connections all over the world, which equates to a new degree of visibility to other jobs, workplace cultures, salaries, and the societal impact of organizations.

This elevates the importance of story within the organization, as people are increasingly leaving jobs when they do not feel connected to the company's mission, values, or leadership.

Story also has an impact on recruiting. When I was considering working for Underwriters Laboratories (UL), I looked into its history and was excited at the prospect of being a part of an organization whose founder had been hired to examine the safety of the electrical wiring in the Palace of Electricity in the 1893 Chicago World's Fair, one of the last stages in the war of the currents between Edison and Westinghouse. My interest grew when I read on and learned that in the early days of electricity, whole city blocks were burning down before UL developed standards that quietly set the stage for the safety we take for granted in the twenty-first century. When I learned that UL was privately held, controlled by a nonprofit focused on safety, security, and sustainability, I was sold. I was so excited about the stories around the company that I recruited a friend of mine to join the company with me, and convinced him to join on the basis of the same set of stories and what I had observed about the organizational culture throughout the interview process. He started a few months after I did.

Within the organization, the pride associated with its impact on and place in history was palpable, together with stories about delighting in the process of applying science to test and certify products for safety before they go to market.

The stories at technology companies, which do not all have the same luxury of longevity, are based on symbols for shared values and identity, often tied to the tangible work product of the organization. These elements of story and symbolism, represented either physically or virtually, have the power to shape the tone of an organization.

As someone who has held a badge for both Amazon and Microsoft, I have often been asked about the difference between their organizational cultures. What I typically share is that when I worked for Amazon, my experience of the organizational culture was that its intensity was viewed internally as an asset, and took the tone that not everyone could cut it, whereas Microsoft took the tone that emphasized inclusion and empowering everyone within the organization to do their best work.

A story that I often share that is subtle, but representative of the difference between these two organizational cultures, is about the first time I received an email reminder to update my password at Amazon. On the first notification that I received about it being the time of the quarter to update my password, there was a small table that listed the names in my organizational hierarchy up to Andy Jassy, who was then the chief executive officer of Amazon Web Services, with a date by which each leader in the hierarchy would be notified if I failed to update my password.

Microsoft's password update notification, on the other hand, had no such table, and a manager would be notified on the final notification before the deadline. This is a tangible example of how easily a short story—only two paragraphs—can have the potential to color one's perception of two of the most powerful companies in the world. Organizations that recognize the economic value of stories and symbols within their organization are best potential to achieve or retain market leadership in the twenty-first century.

Closing the Story Circle

When an organization espouses a set of values, members of the leadership team must be consistent in their interactions with their team members and in interactions with front-line workers, and they must close the story circle from the boardroom to the front line.

The story circle opens when leaders communicate a vision and a set of values for the organization. The circle is closed when stories from across the organization and from the front line are shared back with the rest of the organization or publicly. This communicates to your organization that you are paying attention, and ultimately that what they do matters.

The opposite of this can be observed in cases when a senior leader shows up for a meet-and-greet that is published broadly, but the senior leader is not interested in hearing from front-line workers or the company is not adequately addressing front-line worker needs.

Most leaders assume they should communicate what is going to happen, but take it to the extreme in an attempt to appear confident and decisive. In the case of the COVID-19 pandemic, many leaders decreed the change. Others communicated the options that had been considered, leadership awareness of employee concerns, various options being considered to address those concerns, and whom to reach out to with any further questions or concerns.

Liz Fosslien, author of *No Hard Feelings: The Secret Power of Embracing Emotions at Work,* shared with me that research shows that if you frame change as an experiment, people are much more willing to adapt. Ironically, many leaders, when attempting to communicate decisively, are actively working against the psychological foundation required for meaningful change.

The application of this lesson in the context of Autonomous Transformation and initiatives involving advanced technologies is that silence from leadership generates uncertainty, which triggers a fight-or-flight response in workers. Organizational leadership teams need to define and communicate their values and their vision for the future of the organization. Once these have been communicated, consistent adherence to those values must be observable and communicated, with organizational directives framed in the context of the ongoing conversation between leadership and the broader organization.

But a conversation between leadership and the organization alone is not enough to shape a social system around stories. This can be observed in the context of political systems, where the top leadership communicates visions and values, but subgroups below the top level of the system maintain subsets of values, shared symbols, and stories in which they find community, identity, and belonging.

Within an organization, if a change is to be accepted in the social system and subsystems of the organization, the same story will need to be communicated differently and by different people. Leaders need to communicate a specific story to board leaders. A different version needs to be crafted for leaders to communicate to managers. Depending on the change, leaders also need to announce to individual contributors, but in parallel, managers need to personalize the story to their teams, appealing to their values and cultural contexts.

Storytelling as an Agent for Change

Investments in storytelling should go beyond executive communications to define an underlying set of frameworks and symbols for sharing ideas (the most formal representation I have observed of this is at Amazon, where written communications such as the "backward press release" and the "6-pager" have become embedded in its social system). This will eliminate wasted time and the untapped potential of additional ideas from across the organization.

In other words, if someone does not get an idea, they cannot give feedback, resulting in a loss of the potential of additional value layered on top of the ideas. This is why most leaders are good storytellers—it is not a result of becoming a leader. Becoming a leader is a result of communicating effectively and rising through the ability to stand on the shoulders of those who have come before or from having benefited from a diverse set of perspectives across the organization.

In the context of future solving and organizational reasoning, it is important, in socializing theories, hypothesis, data, assumptions, and tests for feedback, not to assume there is shared understanding. Immediately after communicating a vision, strategy, or tactical plan, test for understanding and chart it to the level of understanding necessary to get to the desired future.

When communicating across generational or cultural lines, when a label is not resonating with the audience, a story can substitute as a vehicle for the underlying message. When Liz Fosslien gave a copy of her book, *No Hard Feelings: The Secret Power of Embracing Emotions at Work*, to her father, he

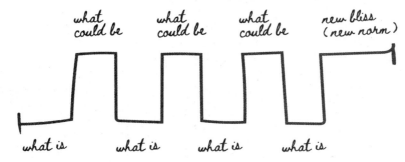

Figure 20.1   Secret Structure of Great Talks by Nancy Duarte

told her he was not sure he would ever understand her generation. After he began reading the book, he called her back and told her that he wished he had understood the concepts she had written about before he retired. The label of emotions mixed with work was anathema to his generational context. The *stories*, however, were relatable and were able to resonate with him.

Nancy Duarte is among the foremost experts on story, communication, and persuasion. In 2022, Nancy was gracious enough to spend 90 minutes with me, and I got to learn firsthand about the power of story and persuasion from her.

A powerful storytelling framework, modeled by Nancy Duarte through analysis of the greatest speeches through history, is called "The Secret Structures of Great Talks" (see Figure 20.1).

When presenting the case for change, whether from a leader to a board, a manager to a team, or an individual contributor with a vision for a new idea within the organization, this storytelling framework can be leveraged after determining an envisioned future ("What could be"), initially by contrasting "What is" with "What could be" to bring others into the organizational reasoning process and subsequently at the onset of each chosen initiative to provide clarity on the purpose of the initiative and to generate momentum and a story around which the social system of the teams assigned to the initiative can form bonds and cohesion.

As Duarte frames it, this begins with understanding who the hero is in a business story. When presenting, the hero is the audience, not the storyteller. When leadership tells stories about culture and initiatives in which they are the heroes, the result is disempowerment and disconnection. When leaders frame stories around initiatives the organization will undergo in the context that the people who make up their organization are the heroes (think nurses and front-line workers during the COVID-19 pandemic), they can light the fuse on meaningful and lasting change across their organizations.

CHAPTER 21

A More Human Organization

I n the wake of the Industrial Revolution and its accompanying mechanistic worldview, organizations have been referred to, designed, and measured as highly complex machines.

The trouble with this view of organizations is that machines are mechanical in nature, and not social, and machines, at the most basic level, are designed and built to execute specifically programmed functions and tasks repetitively.

Humans are social in nature, wildly imaginative, capable of creating meaning and belonging and envisioning the future.

A fully mechanistic future is one in which everything is streamlined, autonomous, and automated.

A more human future is one in which humans, having broken away from the steel chains of the Industrial Revolution, are able to employ the skills with which we have been uniquely gifted to imagine future states in which we would like to exist, create strategies for and subsequently apply ourselves in bringing that future into fruition through acts of creation, reformation, and transformation. Machines, in this paradigm, provide a set of tools for realizing a more human future, as opposed to humans fitting into a more mechanistic future.

The call to transition from a mechanistic worldview to a social systems worldview is not a new one, but in the context of Autonomous Transformation and organizational struggles to realize the economic potential of advanced technologies, together with the broader systemic, societal problems faced by humankind in the twenty-first century, this call has moved from visionary to practical.

Organizations are already social systems, but the majority are not being led and managed as such. The cracks between these worldviews have been widening, such as in the elevation of empathy as a leadership characteristic and the concept of acknowledging, communicating about, and managing emotions in the workplace, both of which have been subjects of *Harvard*

Business Review articles within the past decade. Neither empathy nor emotions equate in a mechanistic system.[1,2]

In the beginning of this book, I drew the distinction that the implementation of advanced technologies within today's context is inextricably tied to creating a more human future, and noted that those who might consider "a more human future" to be impractical will not find the lessons they are looking for in this book (or at least not in the form they anticipated), but that this book is still for them. This paradigm shift, moving from a mechanistic worldview and management approach to a social systems worldview and management approach, presents a path to navigate and lead the complexity of contemporary organizational dynamics, the social and economic systems in which they operate, and the technologies that, unbridled, stand to propel the world toward a more mechanical future.

Through a social systemic lens, social concepts such as diversity, equity, inclusion, belonging, empathy, meaning, Profitable Good, and talent can be more deeply understood and adequately prioritized than through a mechanistic lens.

Once a leadership team, leader, or manager identifies the ways in which they have been managing an organization or team through a mechanistic worldview, the work of transitioning to a social systems leadership style can begin, and the organizational culture can be reformed and transformed into a thriving social system, fit for the purpose of advancing into a more human future.

Experts in fields such as psychology, neuroscience, economics, sociology, organizational design, and human resources, to name a few, have devoted their careers to researching and applying these sciences to organizational leadership and reshaping management both in theory and in practical application within organizations. A list of resources from these experts can be found online at brianevergreen.com/booklist.

Notes

1. S. Barsade, and O. A. O'Neill, "Manage Your Emotional Culture," *Harvard Business Review*, January–February 2016, 58–66.
2. S. Turkle, "Empathy Rules," *Harvard Business Review*, February 17, 2022, https://hbr.org/2022/02/empathy-rules (accessed January 28, 2023).

PART EIGHT

Autonomous Transformation Technologies

Large-scale AI is shifting the landscape of computing research. As we orient around that shift, we'll see new frontiers that advance our understanding of human and machine intelligence and how they can intersect and reinforce each other in profound new ways.

—Ashley Llorens

CHAPTER **22**

Autonomous Transformation Technologies: A Leader's Guide

utonomous Transformation is comprised of five key technologies: artificial intelligence, the Internet of Things, digital twins/simulations, robotics, and virtual and augmented reality.

The first four have each passed their inflection points, demonstrated by organizations around the world setting their strategies and investing in building or buying these capabilities. The inflection points for virtual and augmented reality, on the other hand, will arrive when the right degree of technological advancements and policy enable commoditization in both enterprise and consumer markets. They are included in the scope of Autonomous Transformation because they will become a critical lens through which developments in artificial intelligence, the Internet of Things, digital twins/simulations, and robotics can be observed, collaborated on, managed, and operated.

As with all new or reimagined technologies, the technologies of the era of Autonomous Transformation are best defined through examples. The following are three vignettes, with increasing complexity, to highlight the interplay and possibilities of these technologies.

I provide the caveat up front that the lines between Digital and Autonomous paradigms, as well as between Reformation and Transformation, are blurred, and that I am using Autonomous to describe the accumulated capability of several technologies that could also be leveraged to transition from the analog to digital paradigm without creating autonomy.

Autonomous Transformation Example 1: Product Development

The design, development, building, and scaling of a physical product is a complex process with many steps and organizations involved. Even a product as simple as a lamp still requires design, proof-of-concept, testing, regulatory approval, and suppliers for each component, the simplest of which contains nine components.

An analog version of the design process starts with sketches and drawings, including tables and figures of specifications such as width, diameter, length, voltage, and many more. This design would then be reviewed by manufacturers to determine the feasibility of manufacture and which components and materials would need to be purchased from suppliers, followed by subsequent research to determine suppliers and to design logistics, cost assessments to determine profitability of the product, patent applications, and submission to regulatory authorities for approval to sell within targeted jurisdictions—to name a few of the necessary steps. It is a lengthy, complex process.

Digital Reformation and Transformation have increased the speed of reviews and materially changed the design process through the addition of digital design capabilities. Digital advancements have enabled designers all over the world to collaborate in real time, and have significantly reduced the effort required to research suppliers and to model logistics. Digital capabilities have also created greater insights into past performance across verticals to inform cost/benefit analyses and have simplified the execution of cost modeling and testing scenarios.

Autonomous Transformation takes an additional step forward. The design can be built as a first-principles ("true-to-physics") simulation (i.e., a digital twin of the proposed product), which serves as a bridge between the physical and digital paradigms. This can then be tested for feasibility of manufacture based on digital twins of the organization's factories and machines. If, for example, the product called for an eight-foot metal arm bent at a degree that was not feasible for any of the machines in the factories, this hindrance could be caught without the need for human review. Generative artificial intelligence could then be used to propose design considerations that could achieve a similar design aesthetic while achieving feasibility based on existing and planned manufacturing capabilities.

In terms of cost modeling, the Internet of Things in the factories, consisting of cameras and sensors, would have collected troves of information on quality defects, the patterns of which could be analyzed against the new design to find correlations and propose design considerations that could lower the likelihood of defects and therefore waste. This would improve the profitability calculation. The Internet of Things data could also include information on downtime, changeover, and efficiency in the development of products, which, paired with digital twins of the machines that would be used to make the product, would create more realistic cost and yield estimates than were previously possible. A digital twin of the existing supply chain and logistics could be leveraged for examining new suppliers and identifying options for fulfillment from existing suppliers, such as increasing an order for a specific type of steel from a known supplier. If it was determined that a new supplier would be necessary, artificial intelligence could recommend suppliers based on logistical, geopolitical, cost, quality, and ethical considerations and subsequently model the logistical path.

The accumulated digital representation of the entire product design developed through this process could then be submitted to regulatory authorities who could perform physics-based simulated tests on the design to narrow the scope of necessary physical tests, increasing the product's speed to market.

The digital model developed through this process would continue to add value in future scenarios, such as monitoring the quality of supplier materials and components. Artificial intelligence could comb through defect data supplied by sensors and cameras from the Internet of Things as well as from product returns, recalls, or sensors embedded in the product to find correlations between components supplied and deficiencies or strengths in quality. Another application of the model after the design and approval phase would be in a scenario such as the need to reduce cost by 2% that was posed in a previous chapter. In this case, artificial intelligence could be leveraged to propose design considerations to reduce cost, taking into account aesthetics, quality, technical specifications, and digital twins of the factories. Using aluminum instead of steel, for example, might have appeared to be worth consideration to a human designer in the analog process, but would be eliminated from consideration in moments by artificial intelligence due to the temperatures required to harden aluminum to the technical specifications, which might not be possible with the organization's machine capabilities. This is an example of two key principles of Autonomous Transformation in action: the harnessing of human expertise across disciplines through technology, and augmenting the human creator to increase the ability to execute on existing workloads and extend capabilities into new workloads.

The remaining Autonomous Transformation capabilities that play into this process are robotics and virtual and augmented reality. Augmented and virtual reality play a similar role in this context, in visualizing the product for new designers, visualizing and supporting creative changes through the design process, and visualizing failure points within the context of the completed product for manufacturing engineers and operators. The state of robotics within the Digital Transformation paradigm has begun the shift from human engineers spending hours calibrating a machine to perform a task to using artificial intelligence capabilities to allow the robot to experiment and learn safely in a digital environment, thereby reducing the human effort required as well as time. In the Autonomous Transformation paradigm, this progresses into programming human expertise through machine teaching, which provides curricula within which the machine can train. This has been demonstrated to reduce the amount of experimentation and self-learning required by the machine by 45 *times* the undirected reinforcement learning approach, achieving significant cost reductions and unlocking use cases previously unavailable to machines due to the required nuance.[1]

Autonomous Transformation Example 2: Global Logistics

At any given moment, millions of goods are being moved from one location to another by car, van, truck, railroad, ship, or airplane. These include everything from chemicals, metals, batteries, and food to clothing and *Star Wars* collectibles purchased on eBay. A single bottle of hand sanitizer required the harvesting and shipping of chemicals to a manufacturer, which then manufactured, bottled, boxed, and shipped the hand sanitizer to stores all over the world.

Going into the analog world of global logistics may be too far back, as that included horses and telegraph communications and, later, fax machines. Digital Transformation's largest impact on logistics is communication. The current state of progress, broadly speaking, is that a material or good (down to the SKU, or stock keeping unit) can be tracked live anywhere around the world. This means that a retailer can see that the shipment of their bestselling sweater that they were hoping to restock is actually going to be approximately three days late and is on a freight sailing across the Pacific Ocean, and they should end the flash sale earlier than planned so as not to run out of stock.

A reimagining of global logistics in the era of Autonomous Transformation starts with a digital model of the planet, or at least of every logistical path. What is currently directional and reliant on crowdsourced updates for directions and estimated travel times for consumers is not reliable for enterprises because it is not possible to crowdsource updates about fallen timber over railway tracks in a remote mountain. The Internet of Things creates the possibility for sensor data to be tied to the digital twin of the logistical path of each individual item. Visibility into areas of the logistical route that are unmonitored by the cameras or sensors could adjust calculations, estimates, and pricing in real time. Partnerships with airlines, the use of drones, and purchases of satellite imagery for the areas where camera monitoring is not possible would create a method of ensuring that landslides, fallen trees, and other detectable issues are caught and addressed before they become emergencies.

Artificial intelligence can be leveraged to perform simulations of various groupings of items to determine the fastest fulfillment path and prioritizing premium shipping and guaranteed arrival dates.

When disaster does strike, artificial intelligence could determine the quickest and most cost-efficient path for each item to get to its destination and reroute the packages and assignments accordingly.

Robotics are already being used in warehousing contexts, but as mentioned earlier, they will now be able to address previously unaddressable use cases—in this case, the picking and packaging of goods. Drones will be able to explore physical blockers with the potential to develop capabilities to remove blockers, such as finding a tree and requesting a fleet of drones that are able to lift and move the tree without the requirement of human intervention. As many have likely seen in the news, innovations are also being explored to leverage drones for delivering individual packages to consumers. Merck is a great example of this, as they have developed capabilities for delivering medication to those for whom a disruption in medication would be dangerous when a natural disaster disrupts the preexisting supply chain.[2]

Virtual reality can play a critical role in connecting supply chain analysts and decision-makers with the real context of disruptions, effectively transporting them into the situation to understand the full context. This will reduce organizational friction by creating proximity, and a deeper understanding will enable more effective and creative collaboration.

Autonomous Transformation Example 3: Health Care

Autonomous Transformation empowers consumers and the organizations that serve them to increase proximity through digital means. In health care, Digital Transformation has transformed physical records to digital records. Notes and summaries from appointments, surgeries, or treatments can be accessed online, and prescriptions can be managed and requested online. Doctors can also now access records across hospitals, and the advent of telehealth appointments means that checkups and nonurgent issues can be addressed from the comfort of a patient's home.

Health care through an Autonomous Transformation lens, to expand on the example at the beginning of this book, would start with creating a digital twin of a patient's body. All known allergies, surgical records, hospitalizations, diagnoses, genetic history, medications, and symptom records would create a rich digital twin upon which analyses could be performed. The questions that patients currently answer each time they see a new specialist or doctor, or the time spent by the health care provider in reviewing previous doctors' notes, could be significantly reduced. Previously intangible nuances such as pain tolerance could be captured as baselines for pain medications can be established and dynamically remodeled across visits, surgeries, and hospitalizations. Artificial intelligence layered on top of this digital model could interact with the doctor, who could posit a hypothetical diagnosis or treatment to the machine for feedback. If, for example, the doctor were considering whether the patient had an iron deficiency due to his symptoms, she could input that hypothesis for feedback, and the machine could share recent blood work results, cross-check for iron deficiencies in the patient's familial records, and order bloodwork if there was insufficient data to be able to draw a conclusion. These accumulated digital models could be reviewed by doctors and patients in family planning to ensure that the family and health care team are monitoring for likely complications based on family history. For example, if a pregnant patient and her grandmother and father all suffered from complications stemming from a rare genetic deviation through the toddler years and into early youth, it would be likely that her children would be faced with the same complications. If she did not remember the exact issue she faced, or perhaps misunderstood it to be due to a different cause (which is not at all uncommon), the condition could go unmonitored and unmitigated in her child. The burden of remembering medical details of family histories can be shifted from nonmedical individuals to digital models accessible to a patient's care team.

This technological shift would also reduce the pressure on doctors to ask all the right questions during patient visits, with the potential to transform the process of reviewing documentation before and after visits to be more focused and efficient. During overnight stays, the digital model of patient pain threshold, personal baselines for vital signs, comfort levels, and allergies, for example, would augment nursing capabilities to assist with reducing the load on nurses, especially in the context of staffing shortages.

Proposed interventions such as prescriptions or surgeries could first be run in a science-based simulation of the patient to predict likelihood of success and generate insights of potential strengths and weaknesses. A readout of this accumulated model and analyses could also be shared with insurance companies to justify chosen medical interventions.

The Internet of Things in this context could contribute significantly to the dynamism of the model. Adding heart rate, movement, calories, and exercise information would indicate the individual's level of wellness, and could create opportunities for patients to be proactively notified of unusual heart activity. This is already in the market with fitness trackers and watches, but could take a step further through integration with an accumulated digital model of an individual's broader wellness, medications, history, and genetics to generate alerts and insights more personalized for the individual that then could be shared with a medical team if the individual chose to pursue medical intervention.

Virtual and augmented reality, in this context, can create the ability for medical professionals to collaborate in a new fashion, viewing three-dimensional models of a patient's organs, scans, joints, or fractures. A plan of reasoning and action could then be documented digitally, the output of which could be personalized to each medical professional based on their disciplines and personal preferences. One surgeon might want to review a three-dimensional model and simulation prior to performing surgery. Another might want to use augmented reality during the surgery to keep track of vitals, the plan, and to account for any anomalies.

From a robotics perspective, as robotics are increasingly used in various medical interventions, digital models, combined with artificial intelligence (specifically, deep reinforcement learning, for the technologists reading this), could serve as the input to a machine task. This, paired with using machine teaching to capture human nuance in the medical context, could greatly augment medical professionals and assist with the higher degree of demand than available supply of medical professionals and expertise.

This example is much more uncomfortable for the average reader and for technologists to discuss, because health care strikes to the most fundamental level of existence: life itself. Beyond personal comfort levels with the subject, there is the added complexity of a heavy degree of regulation (and for good reason), as well as privacy concerns.

This illustrates another key element of the era of Autonomous Transformation. The technological capabilities that comprise this era can only be harnessed in the context of new overarching systems: of the health care system, the health insurance system, the educational system, health care policies, and the broader ecosystem supporting health care. Transformations of this nature are critical and inevitable given the advancements of technology and society. Leaders have the opportunity, at the onset of this new era, to design the transformation to achieve a more human future.

A Note on Blockchain

Blockchain is an important technological advancement, and a critical enabler for the next iteration of the decentralized World Wide Web (Web 3.0). Although it is not a core technological component of Autonomous Transformation, it can be leveraged in combination with Autonomous Transformation technologies to engender trust within organizations, between organizations, and between organizations and consumers.

Within the context of the global logistics example discussed earlier, blockchain could be leveraged to provide visibility to the chain of custody between organizations and to the consumer. A layer deeper than logistics is in the actual sourcing of materials, goods, and labor involved. This is one of the key arenas in which explorations and investments in blockchain are taking place, with the aim of creating and maintaining certifiably ethical sourcing.

The health care example almost necessitates a discussion about blockchain. Currently, individual health care records are distributed across systems within every health care provider a patient has visited. Each hospital, insurance provider, pharmacy, and medical laboratory has at least one record stored in a database, whether on premises or in the cloud. This redundancy renders maintaining current records across all systems practically impossible, and, more importantly, decreases both the privacy and security of important personal data.

Decentralizing this information would remove redundancies and provide patients with full visibility to their medical records. At the point at which a provider needed to access medical information in order to examine or treat a patient, the patient could leverage their private key, review the access level requested, and grant the provider access to the blockchain for a designated period of time, which the patient could revoke at any time. Any new information added by the health care professional would be signed by his or her personal key, which would mean that patients would not have the ability to alter information without the approval and participation of the medical professional who entered that information. This would be important for maintaining the integrity of medical records.

Blockchain, much like the technologies within the scope of Autonomous Transformation, has tremendous capability to advance progress and contribute to the creation of a more human future, but in order to achieve its potential, it will require systemic design, the creation of Profitable Good market dynamics, and surprising and remarkable partnerships.

Notes

1. A. Gudimella, R. Story, M. Shaker, R. King, M. Brown, V. Schnayder, and M. Campos, "Deep Reinforcement Learning for Dexterous Manipulation with Concept Networks," submitted September 20, 2017, https://doi.org/10.48550/arXiv.1709.06977.
2. S. Balasubramanian, "Merck Is Piloting a Drone Delivery Program for Medications," *Forbes*, October 26, 2020, https://www.forbes.com/sites/saibala/2020/10/26/merck-is-piloting-a-drone-delivery-program-for-medications/?sh=7843566459b8.

CHAPTER 23

A Deeper Dive into Artificial Intelligence

The story of artificial intelligence began in 1956. Researchers and academics set out to achieve the impossible for the betterment of humankind. Over the years, artificial intelligence has been met with optimism, skepticism, falling in and out of the public eye, and in the past decade has risen to join the most prominent topics of modern discourse.

For some, it poses the greatest threat to humankind of the twenty-first century. For others, it holds the promise of improving the human experience and addressing some, if not many, of the world's biggest challenges.

These points of view could not be more disparate, and yet they represent a small glimpse into the wide variety of discussions taking place in the media, boardrooms, academic halls, at whiteboards, and across industries and social classes about artificial intelligence. Job loss. Job creation. Economic potential. Reshoring. Universal basic income. The end of humanity. Lights-out factories. Ethics. Responsibility. Bias. Augmenting human potential.

At its core, it is a story of humans and machines. It begins with the question of what it means to be human, and as machines have evolved and their prevalence in modern life has increased, artificial intelligence has become the symbolic figurehead of the machine element in this story of humans and machines.

The Components of Artificial Intelligence

There is a significant degree of semantic satiation facing artificial intelligence and interchangeable references to analytics, statistics, data science, machine learning, reinforcement learning, and autonomous artificial intelligence (to name a few). There are many great resources and technology leaders endeavoring to provide clarity on this topic. If you are a technologist looking for the definitive guide to the technical nuances of this field and its related disciplines, my colleagues and peers in the technology industry have published books, articles, and research papers that speak to that technological, domain-specific altitude. The goal of this chapter is to describe each discipline within and closely related to the field of artificial intelligence at the accessible-with-guidance altitude for business and industry leaders. By the end of this chapter, you as a leader should be able to decipher the difference between each. Figure 23.1 provides a visual reference.

Analytics

Analytics is the systematic computational analysis of data. It is used for the discovery, interpretation, and communication of meaningful patterns in data. There are four categories of analytics: descriptive, diagnostic, predictive, and prescriptive.

Descriptive Analytics: What does my data tell me has happened/is happening?

Much like it sounds, descriptive analytics provides a description of the data, often within a specific period of time, or broken down by category. This type of analytics is the most basic, as it only requires the aggregation, sanitization, and interpretation of data as text or visualization. An example would be a visualization of sales revenue by product in a given month.

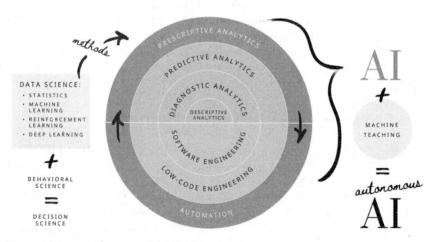

Figure 23.1   Components of Artificial Intelligence

Diagnostic Analytics: Why does my data say that it happened/is happening?

Diagnostic analytics combines several points of analysis together with synthesis, examining data to generate and test hypotheses to illuminate why a particular event occurred or is occurring. Why are sales down? Without diagnostic analytics, an assumption may be made that sales are down because the sales teams are not performing, but a dashboard including diagnostic analytics would be able to introduce the hypothesis that, for instance, customers are not converting from the trial plan to the premium plan because of the high number of incidents and latencies they are experiencing. Synthesis in this context requires an understanding of the domain, which therefore requires the domain expert. There are many organizations that have found that balance within diagnostic analytics through persistent trial and error, but it should be noted that the formal definitions of diagnostic analytics from credible and widely acknowledged resources do not include any references to synthesis, and most explanations of the process only mention the need for technical resources.

Predictive Analytics: What does my data tell me is likely to happen in the future?

Predictive analytics provides predictions of what may happen in the future. For example, based on a high number of incidents and latencies, leading to a reduction in usage from high-paying customers, one can predict the likelihood that those customers will churn. This analytic method is only capable of predicting what may happen in the future if the context of the future is the same as the context from which the data was sampled. An example of this can be observed in the case of predicting churn based on the number of incidents and latencies and decreases in usage; the model does not account for the entrant of a new competitor or an economic downturn.

Prescriptive Analytics: What do my data and business logic tell me I should do next?

Prescriptive analytics prescribe actions based on predictive analytics paired with business logic. To continue in the sales analogy, an example of prescriptive analytics would be assignments in a customer relationship management (CRM) system for salespeople to proactively reach out to customers who, based on a predictive analysis, have a high likelihood to churn. A step further would be a prescriptive recommendation that salespeople offer those customers temporary pricing discounts due to the latencies they have experienced. Without prescriptive analytics, this analysis would have to be done by a consulting firm or an internal team over the course of several weeks or months, and often as a point-in-time exercise. Prescriptive analytics changes this paradigm to predictive analytics that run constantly in the background, searching for patterns when sales numbers start to dip or as soon as a customer begins churning, providing recommendations to business, industry, and technology leaders as soon as they recognize meaningful patterns.

These categories of analytics form an ecosystem that depends on each other's answers to continue to grow and add value. If leaders learn that customers are likely to churn, but they are not provided an explanation as to why or what can be done about it, they will not be able to take informed action to resolve the situation.

Statistics, machine learning, deep learning, reinforcement learning, and other branches within the field of artificial intelligence are methods by which these four categories of analytics can be performed. Machine learning, for example, is often conflated with predictive analytics, but one of the applications of machine learning, classification, can be used to separate customers into categories, thus answering a descriptive analytics question: What are the logical categories of this business's customers based on x, y, and z parameters?

Statistics

Statistics, as defined by the Merriam-Webster dictionary, is "a branch of mathematics dealing with the collection, analysis, interpretation, and presentation of masses of numerical data."[1] At first glance, this is similar to the definition of analytics. The key distinction lies in the process, as indicated in the first portion of the definitions of analytics and statistics. Analytics is "the systematic computational analysis of data" and statistics is "a branch of mathematics dealing with [. . .] data."

In other words, statistics is a method by which analytics can be performed. A data analyst who is not a statistician can identify meaningful patterns in data, such as a decline in profitability, and can pose hypotheses as to the reason, but may not be able to draw definitive conclusions, depending on the complexity of the underlying data. In partnership with a statistician, however, who can test those hypotheses using statistical (i.e., mathematical) models, conclusions can be drawn with enough confidence to inform decisions.

Statisticians who have the skills of analysis and synthesis and can speak the language of the business and/or industry are elite team members, as they can pose meaningful questions, focus their analyses on business objectives, and communicate at the universal or accessible-with-guidance altitude.

Statisticians who do not have the skill of analysis, on the other hand, tend to have an orientation toward theory and mathematical methods that can present challenges in interfacing directly with business and industry leaders, as they are less likely to be able to raise the altitude of discussions above the domain-specific language of mathematics. When organizations identify these kinds of team members or candidates, they can pair them with data analysts to handle the hypotheses, give feedback to ensure that the output of analyses will meaningfully inform decisions, and create effective communications translating the output of those analyses into the accessible-with-guidance altitude.

Data Science

Data science was introduced as a new concept by Chikio Hayashi in 1998, defined as "not only a synthetic concept to unify statistics, data analysis and their related methods but also [comprising] its results. It includes three phases, design for data, collection of data, and analysis on data."[2] Although the discipline and its subfields—analytics, statistics, and machine learning—have evolved considerably since 1998, its focus has remained the same: to derive value out of data.

According to a Gartner research paper, as of 2018, there were only 10,000 scientists worldwide. This figure is staggeringly low, especially when contrasted with the 400 million businesses worldwide, not including the number of public organizations or research and academic institutions.[3] Based on the number of businesses alone, if each could only hire a single data scientist, that means that .000025% of businesses could employ a data scientist.

Organizations around the world have been scrambling to solve this problem. Bootcamps have sprung up, offering to teach data science and assist in landing an entry-level data science job in a number of months. General Electric has addressed this challenge by reengineering the Six Sigma model to fit the discipline of data science, where a "black belt" data scientist can train a number of green belts (typically self-elected from a group of process experts) to drive cost out of operations. The team's success is measured against a targeted cost reduction number.

Cloud providers are attempting to help address this problem by creating increasingly simplified tools to empower elite data scientists to be more effective and junior data scientists to be supported by technological guardrails as they develop their skills and expertise. They are also bundling common data science scenarios, such as object detection within an image, into off-the-shelf services that can be leveraged by software developers.

In addition, new capabilities are being developed that focus on democratizing data science tasks to enable "data science–adjacent" experts in engineering, typically with advanced degrees, to incorporate data science into their work by abstracting the algorithms from the view of the engineer. Machine teaching (discussed later in this chapter) is a new methodology with this focus.

For the purpose of defining data scientists within the list of fields and disciplines in this chapter, a data scientist is an analyst, statistician, and machine learning practitioner. Data scientists are generally capable of building all of the components of artificial intelligence except the automation of the prescribed actions. At this point of the process, data scientists partner with engineers to pair data science with automation to implement artificial intelligence.

If a retail leader, for example, wanted to test different storefront displays and sales advertisements across geographies, a data science team could build the analytical models, data pipelines, dashboards, and prescriptive models to analyze outcomes of these tests and recommend changes to individual stores, analyzing the subsequent results, and further refining those recommendations in a continuing loop of testing and optimization. Partnership with software engineering would come into play when confidence in the prescriptive recommendations reached a point that the business leaders wanted to implement automated prescriptive directives to store leaders—in other words, an artificially intelligent storefront advertising optimization system. Software engineers would then build automation around the prescriptive analytics by devising an alert system through whichever channels would be most efficient for the business. This could take the shape of automated emails, alerts within an application that store leaders were already using, or the creation of a new application to house this specific function.

Decision Science

Decision science combines data science with the behavioral sciences, such as economics, management, neuroscience, and psychology. It takes data science a step further through the orientation of not only optimizing a recommendation that would inform a decision, but also including the science of decision-making within its scope. Extending the storefront example above to include decision science would expand the scope to include analyses such as the science of decision-making of consumers, the economics of the local area, factoring the managerial effect on employees of rotating storefront displays into the cost/benefit analysis, and psychological impacts on customers of various colors in the storefront. This is a relatively new field with exciting implications for combining the richness of the behavioral sciences, previously relegated solely to human expertise, together with data science to create more meaningful and ethical analyses and outcomes.

Decision science is a practitioner's discipline shifted away from a purely mechanistic worldview to a social systems worldview.

Machine Learning

Machine learning is a data science technique that allows computers to use existing data to forecast future behaviors, outcomes, and trends. By using machine learning, computers can learn without being explicitly programmed. Machine learning engineers explore datasets with algorithmic approaches such as deep learning, neural networks, and random forests. A key distinction between a machine learning engineer and a statistician is that the machine learning engineer relies on the algorithm to *learn* the pattern (hence, machine learning) within the data and to generate its own model for replicating that learning. A statistician, in contrast, designs a model, tests the model to see if it matches the desired outcome, redesigns the model, and so on. In the context of artificial intelligence, the model at the center of the prediction that informs the prescribed decision or action could be either a human-written statistical model or a machine-learned algorithmic model.

As children learn, there are some things they are explicitly taught and some they infer. For example, in the United States, children are often taught the phrase "Stop, Drop, and Roll" in case their clothing ever catches fire. This is in large part because they cannot be afforded the opportunity to test the scenario multiple times to see which approach is most effective without suffering bodily harm. This could be likened to the statistical approach, where a machine is provided a "recipe" for how to properly analyze a dataset to reach the desired outcome. Unlike teaching children about fire safety, the skill of climbing a tree is not explicitly taught or prescribed. Children take iterative approaches, forming their own neural pathways and muscle memories, and developing their own skills. This is similar to the machine learning approach, where machines understand the desired outcome and endeavor to reach that outcome, iterating over existing data or generating synthetic data (more on that in the following section) in order to accomplish the prescribed goal.

Generative Artificial Intelligence (Generative AI)

Generative AI is a subdiscipline of machine learning that identifies patterns between inputs and content, which it can then leverage to generate new content, such as images, text, audio files, or videos. Two of the most well-known applications of generative artificial intelligence both launched across the global stage in 2022: DALL·E 2 and ChatGPT.

In the case of DALL·E 2, it has "learned the relationship between images and the text used to describe them."[4] It generates imagery through the use of a technique referred to as "diffusion." This method involves the initial presentation of a random set of dots, which is progressively altered toward the intended image. More specifically, a diffusion model, inspired by non-equilibrium thermodynamics, adds random noise (or "dots") to data and then reverses the diffusion process to construct the desired image from the noise. Although the analogy is not an exact match, this is analogous to a painter dousing their canvas with thousands of little dots, then being able to remove and add individual dots until they reached the desired image.

An important distinction in the discussion around DALL·E 2 and other generative AI models that generate images is that they are only able to replicate patterns based on existing imagery and artistic styles. When Salvador Dali painted his surrealist masterpiece, *The Persistence of Memory*, featuring a new imagining of melting clocks, he was expressing ideological principles based on a writer and poet's definition of surrealism through painting. Generative AI can create new imagery in the style of Salvador Dali or Caspar David Friedrich, but it does not invent new styles of painting or imagery based on ideological principles or personal expression. This remains a distinctly human trait.

ChatGPT is a Large Language Model (LLM) based on GPT that engages in written conversational dialogue and can appear surprisingly human. It was trained on a massive amount of data, at 175 billion parameters and 570 gigabytes of text.[5] One of the aspects that sets ChatGPT apart from traditional LLMs is that it was also trained using human feedback (a technique called Reinforcement Learning with Human Feedback) so that the AI learned what humans expected when they asked a question. Training the LLM this way enabled the model to break away from the rut of predicting the next word.

The hype surrounding ChatGPT provides rich examples of the perceived value of technological breakthroughs, as well as the need to continuously clear the digital fog by separating truth from speculation, identifying logical fallacies, and discerning the credibility and trustworthiness of advisors. There will be another excellent opportunity for navigating digital fog with each new version of GPT or similar advancements from other organizations.

Reinforcement Learning

Reinforcement learning is among the most exciting developments of the past decade, and has paved the way for machines to learn without historical data. Imagine if leaders, after presenting their plan to the board, could hit restart and try again an infinite number of times until they perfected the outcome. This is reinforcement learning in layman's terms. A scenario is defined, along with positive and negative reinforcements for various outcomes, and the machine is set loose, exploring the space and starting over as soon as it finds a path that would determine a positive or negative reinforcement. After thousands, hundreds of thousands, or even millions of iterations, depending on the complexity of the scenario and the platform, the machine either indicates the degree of progress it has made and gives its programmer the option to stop, or has learned an optimal path to achieving the desired outcome consistently without explicit directions. An example of this is *Mario*. Imagine explicitly programming *Mario* to beat a single level. Go forward x steps, jump, now go forward, now duck, now jump forward y steps, and so on. Reinforcement learning replaces this with experimentation and often identifies paths that surprise humans. This is how AlphaGo was able to beat the reigning human champion in the game of *Go*, not by analyzing previous games, but by playing millions of games against itself. This technology can also be used to test net-new scenarios to determine the best path forward.

An example of reinforcement learning paired with robotics is in learning a new task. The grasp-and-stack task is a common training and proving ground for new technologies. A robotic arm reaches out, grasps the block, lifts the block, positions it over a stack of other blocks, and places it gently down on top of the stack. The traditional engineering approach to this problem would require a significant investment of a human engineer's time, with precise directional calculations including factors such as velocity, arc, rotation, and stability. The reinforcement learning approach to the same problem is defining the state, or the physical properties of the robot, the block, and the stack, setting the goal, and determining the positive and negative reinforcements (the reward function). While the engineer attends to other tasks, the machine would methodically test various approaches to achieving its goal in a simulated environment. If it knocks the ball over in the virtual environment, that approach is logged as the wrong approach, and the simulation is reset. With the computational power of parallel computing, which allows for a task to share the processing power of many underlying systems, many hundreds of simulations can be run in parallel, updating the shared model at the end of each attempt.

Two key benefits of this technology are the safety afforded by testing in a simulated environment and the lack of dependence on historical data. A significant set of use cases that have not been addressable for previous machine learning methods can now be approached with reinforcement learning.

Autonomous Artificial Intelligence

Autonomous artificial intelligence is easy to conflate with artificial intelligence. The key distinction is found in its application. To return to the retail storefront application, the artificial intelligence solution is in a cycle of continuously learning from feedback loops across all stores, monitoring and tuning to improve outcomes. A central application is stored in the cloud that is then sharing and receiving information back and forth with hundreds of stores. The risk in this solution is extremely low, as an outage in the system would only result in a failure to generate additional recommendations for updating storefront advertising, with no damage to goods or risk to human safety.

Imagine this same approach for landing drones using artificial intelligence. Latency (or data transfer delays) would result in expensive and dangerous crashes. The same approach in manufacturing, if the machine chose to test a slightly different approach, could result in damaging millions of dollars of equipment and danger to humans.

Autonomous artificial intelligence has to be "complete" and its results validated through real-world trials before being placed into production. This does not mean that it cannot continue to be optimized, but the approach to retraining, validation, and deployment are stage-gated due to the higher stakes involved.

Machine Teaching: A New Paradigm

Machine teaching is a technique introduced in 2015 by Microsoft Research. While machine learning is focused on algorithms and improving the ability of machines to learn, machine teaching focuses on the opposite side of the paradigm, namely, the ability of humans to teach machines.

This discipline arose to address the problem mentioned previously in the data science section: there are not enough experts to build machine learning systems based on the current approaches and the requirement of machine learning expertise. The imbalance of the demand for machine learning systems and the ability for organizations to build them is a leading contributor to the high percentage (87%) of data science projects that never make it into production.

Machine teaching provides a methodology for meeting the growing demand for machine learning systems not only by increasing the ability of machines to learn, but by significantly increasing the number of individuals who can teach machines by making the process of teaching machines accessible.[6,7]

There are *10,000 times* the number of domain experts in the world as data scientists. Machine teaching creates the ability for these experts to teach machines with less reliance on data scientists.

There will likely be several approaches to implementing machine teaching. Current applications start with human expertise, defining curricula as if a human were going to teach another human. Simulations are created based on a dataset or a physics-based representation of the machine, environment, or process. Reinforcement learning references the curriculum instead of blindly searching and relying solely on positive or negative reinforcement.

In the previous example of drones, this approach has been used to teach machines using the expertise of pilots. In the example of grasp-and-stack, this approach enabled the machine to learn the task 45 times faster than reinforcement learning without machine teaching. PepsiCo has used machine teaching to teach humans how expert operators make the perfect Cheeto. The system leveraged reinforcement learning with the addition of the curricula set by human experts, and has been tested and certified as an expert-level operator.

Automation versus Artificial Intelligence

Many companies have implemented decision tree–based automation. Call centers, automated checkout machines at grocery stores, robots that grasp and stack items in factories, motion-controlled doors, and ATM machines are all examples of automation, but not artificial intelligence.

Decision tree–based automation is a list of if-then rules. If the customer presses 1, that input directs the next step, and so on. This is "third-industrial-revolution-level" automation, and it is not artificial intelligence. Artificial intelligence, in this example, still references rules and decision trees. The key differences in the artificial intelligence example are machine learning for voice-to-text translation (i.e., the input is enabled by machine learning), machine learning to predict customer lifetime value to determine whether to offer a discount, and the machine having the authority to offer a discount based on the result of this analysis.

There are several definitions of artificial intelligence. The Merriam-Webster dictionary defines artificial intelligence as "a branch of computer science dealing with the simulation of intelligent behavior in computers" or "the capability of a machine to imitate intelligent human behavior."[8] Microsoft's Cloud Computing dictionary defines it as "the capability of a computer system to mimic human-like cognitive functions such as learning and problem-solving."[9] Google describes it as "a field of science concerned with building computers and machines that can reason, learn, and act in such a way that would normally require human intelligence or that involves data whose scale exceeds what humans can analyze.[10]

Automation, on the other hand, is defined by the Merriam-Webster dictionary as "the technique of making an apparatus, a process, or a system operate automatically."[11]

Automation without artificial intelligence is a script composed of decision-trees and corresponding commands programmed by a human. When motion is detected, turn on the floodlights. When I say this command to my digital assistant, turn off all the lights in the house, lock all the doors, and start playing my bedtime playlist.

Artificial intelligence, on the other hand, cannot exist without automation. In the definitions above, you see the words *imitate*, *mimic*, and *act*. Artificial intelligence, broadly speaking, intakes data, applies a statistical model or machine learning algorithm to the data to predict and recommend actions, takes action, then learns from the results of those actions. In other words, artificial intelligence without automation is reduced to predictions and reports, and therefore not actual artificial intelligence.

Automation versus Autonomy

Automation and *autonomy* are often used interchangeably, but they are not the same. Automation, as a set of explicitly programmed instructions, is not possible if either the environment, the input, or any other variables are dynamic. This is when autonomy is required.

Imagine two machines side by side in 2010. One machine cuts stacks of paper into two pieces. The second machine bakes paper. Assuming the output of that baked paper is consistent, the machine that cuts the paper follows approximately four steps:

Step 1: Pull the paper into the machine.

Step 2: Make sure the paper is aligned to the prescribed parameters.

Step 3: Cut the paper.

Step 4: Feed the paper back out of the machine.

There are only a handful of variables in this process and in the paper-cutting machine that could possibly change: the blade could become dull, the system that aligns the paper could get out of alignment, the feeders for pulling paper into the machine or pushing it out of the machine could malfunction. Each of these variables is extremely noticeable, and becomes a matter of repairing the machine, which is addressed by ongoing maintenance. The only real variable is the consistency of the paper fed into the machine.

Now let us examine the machine that makes the paper. This machine ingests raw materials, fits them into a mold, bakes that material into paper, and uses coloring to account for the variability of the pulp. In 2010, this machine and its process must be operated by a person, because there is not another method of managing the variability across all the factors required, such as the humidity taken together with the temperature of the pulp. The coloring of each batch contains so much variability that a human must review the variables, exercise judgment, and learn from the outcome; this is work that cannot be automated into a script. There are too many variables to be taken into account, not to mention unknowns.

Autonomy can be achieved in this scenario by creating a first princi- ples (or "true-to-physics") simulation of the machine and if each batch of pulp was examined first for coloring, then viscosity, then temperature, and so on, together with the humidity in the environment and the expertise of the operators who spent many years, if not decades, fine-tuning their approach, which can be programmed as skills. Deep reinforcement learning can then experiment within the confines of the simulation, executing trial-and-error experiments safely away from the machine and the materials within a digital simulation. Framed by the programmed expertise, it can practice and learn the skill to the degree that it can be certified to run a machine autonomously. This has been demonstrated at PepsiCo, where an autonomous agent has been trained and subsequently certified to run an extruder that makes Cheetos, a process that could never be scripted/automated.[12]

How to Tell When Someone Is Lying about Artificial Intelligence

One of the greatest contemporary societal harms associated with the field of artificial intelligence is in the misrepresentation, through ignorance or malice, of knowledge, applications, or capabilities in artificial intelligence.

An advertisement of a product or technology, in today's market, all but falls flat without the mention of artificially intelligent features. For many dis- cerning leaders, the din around the topic of artificial intelligence has resulted in a degree of skepticism. The economic potential trapped within this para- digm is astounding. Cutting through misinformation around artificial intel- ligence will naturally focus market investments in technologies that are creating powerful and impactful applications of artificial intelligence, and has the power to create more top- and bottom-line revenue, leading to more jobs and greater job security.

The ability to tell whether someone is lying about artificial intelligence can be achieved through the application of two of the concepts introduced previously in this book in combination with one new method.

First, by applying the economic incentive test (Chapter 13), it is possible to gain an understanding of an advisor's credibility and trustworthiness.

The second method for determining a person's credibility in the field of artificial intelligence is through the three altitudes of inputs and outputs framework (Chapter 14). At whichever altitude the discussion lands, introduce the framework and ask the person to adjust the altitude up or down accordingly. An expert in artificial intelligence should be able to transition altitudes, although some may be more clunky in communicating at an altitude in which they are less versed. It should become clear in relatively short order whether the issue is in trying to explain something complex in common language (i.e., they are an expert technologist but not an expert communicator) or whether they are unable to explain anything beyond the verbiage or pitch they have memorized. It should be noted that the latter case reflects on the person communicating, and not necessarily the underlying technology. If the application or capability is intriguing enough to test for further depth, leaders should feel comfortable requesting a technical demonstration and invite technology leaders from within the organization to review the demonstration and probe to verify the technical depth of the team and the solution.

The third method is for leaders to listen closely and ask questions regardless of their knowledge of the answer. Leaders can then pose questions at each ambiguous or inconsistent juncture in the presentation, such as at the mention of "proprietary algorithms" or that a team of data scientists would be needed to implement a solution that has been presented as off-the-shelf. If the presenter is an expert, it presents a learning opportunity. If they are not, it saves the organization time and resources to identify this as early as possible.

Quiz

If you can correctly answer all 10 of the following questions, you will be ready to navigate many conversations around artificial intelligence, ask the right questions, make informed decisions, and start on the journey of building and leading data and decision science teams and machine teaching programs across your business. Additional industry and technology-specific reading can be found at brianevergreen.com/booklist.

1. What percentage of data science projects make it into production?
    (A) 7%
    (B) 42%

(C) 13%

(D) 21%

2. Which type of analytics would best answer the following question: "Why are customers leaving us for our competitors?"
   (A) Descriptive analytics
   (B) Diagnostic analytics
   (C) Predictive analytics
   (D) Prescriptive analytics

3. Which data science subfield involves the fine-tuning of mathematical models to improve predictions?
   (A) Statistics
   (B) Machine learning
   (C) Data mining

4. Which of these examples would be automation, but not artificial intelligence?
   (A) Recommending products online based on usage patterns and demographic information
   (B) Notifying a customer service manager of an agitated customer based on sentiment analysis
   (C) A driver's seat in a car recognizing a specific driver based on their weight and adjusting temperature, steering wheel, and seat orientation to that driver's preferences
   (D) Logging into a phone using facial recognition

5. Which of these examples would be an application of artificial intelligence?
   (A) Alerting factory workers of a chemical spill based on camera feeds
   (B) A chatbot that references a lookup table to answer frequently asked questions
   (C) Auto-filling online forms with name, email, and phone number
   (D) Stopping a manufacturing line when a person gets too close to the machine

6. In which use case would it be necessary to use autonomous artificial intelligence?
   (A) Reviewing sensitive patient data to detect cancer
   (B) Controlling the temperature in an office building
   (C) Playing *Mario*
   (D) Controlling a high-speed machine in a factory

7. Which of these examples extends beyond data science into decision science?
   (A) Predicting the percentage increase in sales that will result from a proposed marketing campaign
   (B) An artificially intelligent chatbot that uses natural language processing to translate technical documentation into customer-friendly language

    (C) Assessing customers for the degree of uncertainty they feel when they see a marketing ad and predicting the resultant impact to sales

    (D) An application that writes poetry in 20 different languages

8. Which use case would be the best for reinforcement learning?
   (A) Breaking customers into categories
   (B) Calibrating a thermal reactor
   (C) Predicting customer churn
   (D) Designing a new shoe based on preexisting shoe designs, sales, and physical and anatomical science

9. Which subdiscipline of artificial intelligence is the most capable of translating human expertise to machines?
   (A) Machine learning
   (B) Statistics
   (C) Decision science
   (D) Machine teaching

10. If a business has never analyzed any of their data and is just getting started, whom should they hire first?
    (A) A data scientist
    (B) A decision scientist
    (C) A data analyst
    (D) A machine learning engineer

    Answers: C, B, A, C, A, D, C, B, D, C

Notes

1. "Statistics," Merriam-Webster Dictionary, https://www.merriam-webster.com/dictionary/statistics (accessed February 11, 2023).
2. C. Hayashi, C. (1998). "What Is Data Science? Fundamental Concepts and a Heuristic Example," *Data Science, Classification, and Related Methods: Studies in Classification, Data Analysis, and Knowledge Organization*, edited by C. Hayashi, K. Yajima, H. H. Bock, N. Ohsumi, Y. Tanaka, and Y. Baba (Tokyo: Springer, 1998), https://doi.org/10.1007/978-4-431-65950-1_3.
3. Dun and Bradstreet, "D&B Data Cloud Surpasses 400M Businesses," press release, November 5, 2020.
4. OpenAI, DALL·E 2, https://openai.com/dall-e-2 (accessed February 22, 2023).
5. A. Tamkin and D. Gangul, "How Large Language Models Will Transform Science, Society, and AI," Stanford University, Human-Centered Artificial Intelligence, February 5, 2021, https://hai.stanford.edu/news/how-large-language-models-will-transform-science-society-and-ai (accessed February 22, 2023).
6. J. Carter, "Going beyond Data Scientists: What Is Machine Teaching?," *Techradar*, August 11, 2015, https://www.techradar.com/news/world-of-tech/going-beyond-data-scientists-what-is-machine-teaching-1301201/2 (accessed February 24, 2023).

7. Gudimella et al., "Deep Reinforcement Learning for Dexterous Manipulation with Concept Networks."

8. "Artificial intelligence," Merriam-Webster Dictionary, https://www.merriam-webster.com/dictionary/artificial intelligence (accessed 24 February 24, 2023).

9. Microsoft Azure, "What Is Artificial Intelligence?," https://azure.microsoft.com/en-in/resources/cloud-computing-dictionary/what-is-artificial-intelligence (accessed February 24, 2023).

10. Google Cloud, "What Is Artificial Intelligence (AI)?," https://cloud.google.com/learn/what-is-artificial-intelligence (accessed February 26, 2023).

11. "Automation," Merriam-Webster Dictionary, https://www.merriam-webster.com/dictionary/automation (accessed February 26, 2023).

12. Leah Culler, "More Perfect Cheetos: How PepsiCo Is Using Microsoft's Project Bonsai to Raise the (Snack) Bar," *Microsoft Blogs*, December 17, 2020, https://blogs.microsoft.com/ai-for-business/pepsico-perfect-cheetos/ (accessed February 26, 2023).

CONCLUSION

We come from a long line of humans endeavoring to make sense of the world, to find and make meaning in creating safety, beauty, and community, and to create a better future for their families and for future generations.

Scientific, social, artistic, and technological creations and breakthroughs throughout history broke through contexts with more constraints and fewer resources than are available to anyone who has the privilege of sitting down to read or write a book in the twenty-first century.

The future is not a trend that can be modeled or that we can or even need to predict. It takes bravery and vulnerability, but within thriving social systems, it is possible to envision and create a more human future.

But we cannot create a more human or better future within mechanistic organizations or by mechanistic methods. The time has come to break out of the local minutiae of the Industrial Revolution. It is time for a decisive, worldwide shift toward a new way of thinking, talking about, approaching, and managing organizations, initiatives, teams, and systems. And it absolutely will not happen organically.

My hope for the context, frameworks, methods, and strategies in this book is that they contribute to a worldwide swing out of the Industrial Revolution and into an era in which organizations and ecosystems become truly human-centered social systems in name, theory, and practice, followed by a form of renaissance, in which the centuries of thought and research related to the social sciences are more fully integrated into all disciplines spanning organizations. The ineffectiveness of attempts to implement artificial intelligence and its adjacent technologies are symptoms of the deeper issue, the resolution of which will lead to harnessing unprecedented economic and social potential, changing the very nature of work for the better, and a brighter future for humanity.

As for me, the next phase of my journey will be focused on helping people and organizations to leverage the frameworks, methods, and strategies in this book for practical application within their organizations, industries, and markets, and partnering with academic and industry leaders to generate research, learnings, and frameworks to extend this body of work, insights, and knowledge.

As for you, regardless of the point at which you find yourself in your career, or with what level of purview and resources, you and your organization are a necessary part of this worldwide transformation. As we have learned in this book, changing the nature of or performance of a part of a system only matters if it influences the performance of the whole system. Together, we can change that system on behalf of future generations. With humility and conviction, and in the face of technological upheaval, we must endeavor to find and use every opportunity to create a more human future for future generations.

WHAT SHOULD YOU READ NEXT?

Always, at the back of your soul, there is something that says to you, "Mortal, drawn from eternal life for a short time, think how precious these moments are."

—Eugene Delacroix

Thank you for taking the time to read this book. Anything you enjoyed in this book is built on the ideas of others who have come before me. Anything you were unsure about or disagreed with is undoubtedly of my own creation.

There are many books I would recommend you read next, broken into categories depending on which section of the book most resonated with you, and if you are more interested in books leaning further in the direction of theory or practice.

This book list is a dynamic document, and can be found at: brianevergreen.com/booklist.

ACKNOWLEDGMENTS

There are leaders all over the world endeavoring to create a more human future, and society is a better place thanks to them. Thank you to everyone who is already working to improve our world and the human experience.

To each of the individuals I have had the opportunity to lead, partner with, work for, and learn from, I want to thank you for being the inspiration and foundation for Autonomous Transformation.

My name may be on the cover of this book, but this book would not have been possible without the leaders I interviewed for this book across the public and private sectors, enterprises large and small, research institutions, and academia. Thank you to Seth, Nancy, Liz, Kim, Reid, Paul, Dan, Tom, Mike, Thorsten, Ragu, Tad, Ellen, Mohan, Heather, Chad, Noelle, Salim, John, Berardino, Ira, Brian, Mark, Jonathan, Tim, Steve, Prabu, Sudhi, Keith, Ron, Andreas, Jeff, Brant, and Bonnie.

My former colleagues at Microsoft were an invaluable resource in sharing their experiences with me and vetting and developing these ideas, and I would like to particularly thank Natasha, Gurdeep, Mark, Keen, Ashley, Somanna, Jennifer, Kence, Hemant, and Wolfgang.

Systems thinking and systemic design are a critical component of this book, and I want to express my deep gratitude to Harold Nelson, Roger Martin, the late Russell Ackoff, and the systems movement for laying the foundation for leaders around the world to see, understand, and design for the complexities of the twenty-first century.

Writing a book one can be proud of is a significant undertaking. The experience is surprisingly existential and vulnerable. I want to thank the individuals who helped make this book happen. Thank you to Sheck, Susan, Philo, and the whole Wiley team.

I want to thank Jacque Vonk, who has been an instrumental collaborator in breathing visual life into the ideas in this book.

Thank you, Audrey Evergreen, for your tireless support in carving out time and space for me to write by moonlight and in vetting, challenging, and refining my ideas. This book would not exist if it were not for you.

INDEX

Page numbers followed by *f* refer to figures.